Westfield Memorial Library
Westfield, New Jersey

W9-CMR-602

How to
Shop
for a
Husband

ALSO BY JANICE LIEBERMAN
(with Jason Raff)

Tricks of the Trade: A Consumer Survival Guide

Westfield Memorial Library
Westfield. New Jersey

How to Shop for a Husband

JANICE LIEBERMAN
with
Bonnie Teller

St. Martin's Press ✹ New York

HOW TO SHOP FOR A HUSBAND. Copyright © 2009 by Janice Lieberman. All rights reserved. Printed in the United States of America. For information, address St. Martin's Press, 175 Fifth Avenue, New York, N.Y. 10010.

www.stmartins.com

Design by Sarah Maya Gubkin
Illustration by William Honkanen

Library of Congress Cataloging-in-Publication Data
Lieberman, Janice.
  How to shop for a husband / Janice Lieberman with Bonnie Teller. — 1st ed.
    p. cm.
  ISBN-13: 978-0-312-54998-5
  ISBN-10: 0-312-54998-9
  1. Mate selection. 2. Women—Psychology. 3. Dating (Social customs)
I. Teller, Bonnie. II. Title.
  HQ801.L467 2009
  646.7'7—dc22

2008043922

First Edition: May 2009

10 9 8 7 6 5 4 3 2 1

To all the girls out there who are shopping for husbands: May your closets be filled with love instead of last year's clearance shoes.

To David, Judah, Alex, and Margaux,
the product of two great shopping trips:
We love you so very much.

And to Steve and Nick: You've made our shopping dreams come true.

Contents

Acknowledgments

Writing a book about husband shopping involves listening to a lot of hilarious and pathetic stories, and also a few wonderful ones. We were lucky enough to have some generous people share their stories with us.

We'd like to thank our dear friends Doryne and Roz not only for sharing their stories, but also for living through ours with us. It was Roz's famous line ("But I don't like his shoes . . . !") that got this all started. Love and kisses also to Kim, Joanne, Shari, Amy R., Jodi, Cecilia, Dana, Shelby, Cuty, Mary, Patty, Amy D., SuSu, Ingrid, Tara, Maggie, Debbie, Jeff, and everyone else who encouraged, listened, and inspired.

Thank you to everyone at the *Today Show,* including Michele Leone, Melissa Pervel, Jackie Levin, and of course to Meredith Vieira and Ann Curry for sharing your stories. Thank you also to Jim Bell for all of your support.

Gracias, Miami, especially to one *very* educated book club, and also to Suzy, Katie, and the girls at RBB Public Relations, without whom we would have been bereft of many a good story indeed.

Thank you to Miriam and Jack for an inspiring story and a great baby name.

We are deeply indebted to all of our experts, including Dale Atkins, Joy Bauer, Laura Berman, Suzanne Bracker, Jean Chatzky, Pauline Coutroulis, Angel de Para, Stacy London, Steve Santagati, Kay Unger, and Laurie Weber.

To artist William Konkanen and photographer Ted Axelrod, you provided the delicious icing for this cake. Thank you.

Love to Charles Grodin. *Mwah!*

To Web geniuses Grace Hanlon and Sarah Powers, you have our gratitude and awe.

To Michael Glantz and Brian Jacobs, television agents extraordinaire: thank you!

Our appreciation to Heidi Krupp, for her promotional expertise.

Thank you to Jeff who dressed me for all those dates. Our gratitude also goes to Diane Miles for her invaluable help.

To Karen Gantz Zahler, thank you, thank you, and thank you for believing in us and making our little idea a reality.

And thank you so much to Elizabeth Beier, Michelle Richter, John Murphy, Ann Day, Tara Cibelli, Jane Liddle, and everyone at St. Martin's, a wonderful place to publish a book.

To Fabiola and Masha, nothing works without you. You have our love and undying gratitude.

To our families, Millie, Marty, Barbara and Audrey, Norma, Danny and Magie, we appreciate your love and support.

To Lizzie, Adam, Noa, and Ava, we thank you for showing us that you can shop early and really, really well.

To Fred and Sidney, you would have gotten a real "kick" out of this.

To Sid, we are so glad you were brought home from the store.

And to Marilyn and Mickey, if you have a great mother, shopping for a husband is easy.

How to
Shop
for a
Husband

Introduction

My friends and I used to have a running joke: we wouldn't date a guy if we didn't like his shoes. I think it was my friend Roz who first pointed out the problem, but then we all fell in line. Geeky shoes were a nonnegotiable no-no, a reason to cross a guy off our unwritten, potential-husband list with no further explanation necessary. If a guy had cheap shoes, shiny shoes, shoes with high heels—pretty much any shoes that weren't black or brown—he was a goner. Ixnay. No go. And you know those worn-out, mousy-brown, sort-of-fuzzy lace-ups? As if!

One by one, my girlfriends managed to get over the shoe thing. They either found guys who wore good-enough shoes, or quickly improved the shoe wardrobe after marriage. My sister managed to find her future husband in summer camp, when they were both sixteen. But there I was, searching endlessly for the perfectly shod man. Looking back, I have to ask myself: was that any way to shop for a husband?

Of course, I had plenty of other reasons besides shoes for crossing guys off my PGHM (Perfectly Good Husband Material) list: boring, bad job, bad breath, bad mother. I have to admit I was kinda picky. There were plenty of pretty nice guys—guys with potential, guys who could, perhaps, have been gently molded into PGHMs—that I dismissed out of hand.

I would say to myself: *shouldn't* a girl be picky? Why should a girl have to settle? And if I do settle, won't I be miserable later on? This internal debate went on for years, while I dated what seemed like most of the eligible bachelors on the eastern seaboard.

There was the doctor who wanted me to room with his mother on vacation. The guy who slurped his yogurt. The ex from high school who always had a new motorcycle but never a job. I dated and dismissed, dated and dismissed, all the while longing for the man with the perfect shoes (and the perfect everything else).

Once in a while I would meet a guy who seemed to be up to snuff, shoes and all. Somehow, though, the relationship would stagnate or stall, and end up going nowhere fast. Maybe, I would console myself, none of these guys was the one meant for me.

But where was he, and why was this so freaking hard?

While my personal life floundered, I have to admit my professional life took off. In fact, the worse things got in the man department, the better they got at the office. Over time I worked my way up from covering stories for a local TV affiliate in Buffalo, New York, to becoming a consumer expert on national network news shows. For years, I anchored a daily TV show on CNBC, *Steals and Deals,* in which we showed the world how not to get scammed. On that show, we offered consumers rules for finding the best products, getting the best deals, and closing those deals on the most favorable terms. Then I joined NBC's *Today Show,* where I became the consumer expert. For a little girl who grew up on

Mary Tyler Moore, I was living the life I had dreamed of, the life I had worked so hard for, the life I so wanted.

But still, no husband. It felt like a big gaping hole in my otherwise very happy life. The bottom line was this: I was a shopping expert, but I didn't know how to shop for a husband.

By the way: does any of this sound familiar to you? I wouldn't be surprised, because most of my girlfriends, not to mention my mother, were in the same boat as I was, adrift in the Sea of No Good Guys. They all had great jobs, great clothes, great friends, and could basically run the world. And they *certainly* knew how to shop. They just couldn't land a good deal on a guy.

After years of dating misery, I finally took matters in hand. After all, this *was* the most important shopping trip of my life, *wasn't it?* And shopping was certainly a topic I knew a lot about. So I decided to approach dating in a smart, systematic way, as if I were making the purchase of a lifetime. Slowly but surely, and almost before I even realized it, I began to apply the rules I had learned as a consumer reporter—caveat emptor, don't get scammed, learn where to shop, and know how to close a favorable deal—to shopping for a husband. I made a list of what I really wanted, I narrowed down the shopping venues to those that would really work for me, I consulted some experts who helped me get into a marriageable state of mind, and I figured out how to close the deal.

As it turns out, shopping for the typical consumer goods— a car, a bed, or a diamond ring—is really not that different than shopping for a guy. The laws of consumer behavior and protection really do apply beautifully to the dating scene. And not long after applying the "rules"—the rules of being an educated consumer, that is—they worked for me. Finally, after years of searching, I met and married Steve, a great guy who even has some really nice shoes. With the recent arrival of our second child, I can't believe I spent all those years not knowing the how, what, and where of shopping for a husband.

I wrote this book because I don't want you to waste time like I did. I'm over it, ladies, and I hope you are, too. Get ready, because in the following chapters, I will show you how to make the rules of consumer behavior work for you in your dating life. After all, it makes sense: dating doesn't need to be the part of your life in which all bets are off and you lose all of your otherwise rational thought processes. No matter how picky you are, you don't need to be the kind of girl who has it all when it comes to her work life, or when it comes to her friends, or even when it comes to her children—but not when it comes to her love life. You don't need to live a life in which your personal happiness is placed firmly on the back shelf with the expired canned goods.

In this book, we will take you through the *entire* husband-shopping process. First, we'll set out the rules for picking out good husband material. What makes for a great, long-lasting relationship and how do we know it when we see it? Then, we'll show you where to shop for that dream guy. Bars, the Internet, singles vacations, your workplace? Which are winners and which are losers? We've got the goods. Finally, we'll give you the inside scoop on closing the deal, and by that we mean ring, aisle, guest list, and honeymoon.

Just follow the rules of being a good consumer, listen to what the experts say, and I think you, too, will be very happy with the "purchase" you make. And you might even like his shoes.

PART I

What to Shop For

We get it. It's easy to get stuck in the "dressing room of dating."

Sure, at first, shopping for a husband can be lots of fun. There are so many different shapes and sizes for a girl to try on! But just like any other shopping trip, if you don't get lucky right away, shopping for a guy can get pretty tiring, pretty fast.

Here's how it usually goes: this one doesn't quite fit around the hips, that one makes you look seriously frumpy, and the other one is waaaaaay too pricey. Before you know it—*can somebody bring me a latte?*—you've tried on more than you can even remember, and you're ready to call it a day. The pile on the dressing room floor has reached mountainous proportions and you've begun to feel as if you'll *never* hear the register go "ka-ching!"

Well, that's where we come in.

Ladies, it's time to shop smart. Just think of us as your very own personal shoppers in this, *the most important shopping expedition of your life.* We're here to teach you how to get a great buy on a guy—and to get you to that checkout counter, pronto.

So, listen up: step number one to becoming a wise shopper in today's dating marketplace, what we call the "meet market," is learning exactly *what to shop for* in a man.

This may seem simple, but believe us, it's not. Finding perfectly good husband material is no easy stroll through the mall these days.

A hundred years ago things were much more straightforward. A girl's parents chose for her, or she selected an eligible man from a small group, narrowly circumscribed by social class, geographic location, and the value of her dowry. Period. This is still the tried-and-true method for finding a spouse in many cultures today, including parts of India, the Middle East, and Japan (although nowadays the arranging often takes place by cell phone and instant messaging). A family meeting, a few chaste dates, and then *wham!* A walk down the aisle.

Are you thinking, *Lucky them?*

We hear you. The state of dating in America today is enough to make a girl wish that the fine art of marriage arrangement weren't a dying practice. A meddling yenta or a courtly coming-out party may sound pretty good if you've become a luckless, long-term Match.com constituent. Okay, sure, a quick perusal of Anna Karenina's or Madame Bovary's miserable marriages will set you straight about the good ol' days, but there is something to be said for rules, criteria, parameters, and traditions when it comes to dating.

Unfortunately, in our world, all bets are off. Here's the harsh truth: it's a free-for-all out there. After all, *anyone* is possible dating material, you can meet that special someone *anywhere,* and when you do, *anything* can happen. Sure, your choices are almost limitless, and the male marketplace is global. This should be a good thing, right? Age, race, and social background may be a consideration, but they are definitely not the insurmountable boundaries they once were. This newfound freedom in dating is not something we're really willing to give up, but it certainly does make dating more baffling than it has ever been.

The questions abound: What *should* you be looking for in a man and *how will you know him when you see him?* What makes a guy a keeper, and who should be tossed out with yesterday's half-eaten Caesar salad?

Okay, no freaking out allowed! Let's think rationally. When the sky's the limit in choosing a husband, then you have to make your own criteria. So, let's look at this as wise consumers:

Q: What do you do when you're setting out on any other important shopping spree?

A: You make a list. A shopping list.

If you're willing to put pen to paper to make a trip to the supermarket, why in the world wouldn't you do it for a husband?

Our advice is this: make a list of the most important characteristics you are looking for in a man. Sounds good, right?

But, wait!

Before you start, read on. We don't want you to make just *any* list. We've seen that one: smart, funny, and handsome. Blah, blah, and blah. Just wake us up when you're done, OK?

We want you to make a list of qualities that really, *truly* count—your very own PGHM (Perfectly Good Husband Material) shopping list—and we're going to help you out.

We've done the legwork for you, ladies, and we've uncovered exactly what it takes to be PGHM. We've also discovered why we women so often don't recognize PGHM when we see it. Let us help you write your very own shopping list that will help you get married to the right guy, on the double.

First, we're going to tell you *why* you are stuck in the dressing room of dating and not hearing the register ring. Then, we'll show you what *really* makes a guy a keeper.

PERSONAL SHOPPER TIP: Check out the PGHM (Perfectly Good Husband Material) Meters throughout Part I of this book—they'll tell you what to look for in a guy. The higher the number on the meter, the better the husband material. Got it? Think of us as *Consumer Reports* meets the *Love Guru*.

Once you learn what really constitutes PGHM, you'll be ready to make your own shopping list in the space provided.

Then you can hit the stores.

You don't have to thank us. It's our pleasure to shop with you!

HERE'S HOW TO SCORE ON THE MEET MARKET

If you want to get out of the dressing room of dating, you have to learn what makes a guy PGHM. Then make your own shopping list and get ready for the most important shopping trip of your life. Before you know it, you'll hear the register go ka-ching!

Rule #1:
Don't Choose a Man by His Shoes—and Don't Be Crazy Picky

Before you can even begin to write your shopping list, you have to understand something about the times in which we live. You've heard of the Greatest Generation, who fought in World War II, and the Lost Generation, who ran off to Paris to write and paint in the 1920s, right? Well, we are the Picky Generation.

Smart marketers know this, and they cash in on it by catering to our every whim. When we go to the supermarket, we can choose from dozens of different types of orange juice, all from the same company. Want pulp? A lot or a little? Extra vitamin C but no calcium? No problem. Calcium but no vitamin C? You got it. You can even have organic, extra-fiber orange juice with antioxidants. Just check the bottom shelf on the left.

Burger King may have started the trend in the seventies when they encouraged us to "have it our way," but could they have envisioned the half-caf, venti, no foam, soy latte with a shot of hazelnut syrup? Actually, would you make that a skinny? Starbucks touts that it is possible to order eighty-seven thousand different permutations of their drinks, with variables that include type of milk, type of sweetener, number of coffee shots, added syrups, and more.

But it doesn't stop at food. iPods allow us to make our own personal playlists, Build-A-Bear lets kids have the special teddy that no one else has, and Dell Computer markets build-to-order computers with specifications that will meet our very own needs and, as we like to tell ourselves, no one else's. The experts call it mass customization, and it appeals to the picky shopper in all of us.

Pickiness is a hallmark of our times and, as *The Washington Post* writer Libby Copeland points out, "There is something peculiarly modern about this phenomenon, something aligned with our dark privilege of too much, this consumeriffic culture in which jeans and houses and breasts and ring tones are customizable."

What does this have to do with dating? Well, our predilection for the personalized, the customized, the made-to-order, and the all-around, generally perfect has bled into our search for a soul mate. Since we can't simply write a recipe for romance, we do the next best thing. We search for the custom-made mate. For example: check out this personal listing from an Ivy League alumni magazine that reads like a wish list written by a very spoiled five-year-old.

Is this guy casting a movie, or is he just plain nuts? We appreciate that he's interested in a woman over fifty and that he's not scared of a facial wrinkle or two, but lots of luck to him in

PICKY PROFILE #1:

MAN LOOKING FOR THE PERFECT WOMAN

Is this you (or someone you know)? Never, ever give up. I can actually picture the perfect woman . . . she's tall, lean, mid-50s, likes to hike and swim in the ocean—and still looks good in a one-piece bathing suit and a Tilley Hat [for those who don't know, like us, that's a broad-brimmed hat made in Canada]. She is sharp-witted, can do the Sunday *New York Times* crossword faster than [me], and has deep laugh lines in her face. She has traveled some, but still has many places she'd like to explore. And she's easygoing. Cooking and cleaning are fine, but she'd rather walk the dog or spend time over wine with friends. She is no patsy; likes to have a good argument to get the juices flowing. She's tough but loving. Oh, and she can remove a snake from a cistern. She's out there. [She should also be] a nonsmoker [and] should be willing to consider relocating to—or at least living half the year in—Australia. Please reply with photos.

finding an Ivy-League, easygoing, snake-killer who is no patsy and wants to move to Australia. We say, Dude! Get real!

But Don Juan Dundee is not alone. Take a look at the "What I'm Looking For" litanies on any online dating site and you'll see what we mean, and ladies . . . don't snicker . . . you are just as bad, if not worse. Check out this recent posting on a dating Web site of a woman in her thirties looking for a man:

PICKY PROFILE #2

WOMAN LOOKING FOR THE MAN OF HER DREAMS

Am looking for a cool, funny, ambitious, intelligent, charming, charismatic, captivating guy...who has a *great* personality and is good-looking and tall...(seriously is this too much to ask for haha). admittedly, i do set my standards high, but i feel as though i have a lot to offer as well, so would not ask for anything i could not reciprocate. overall, however, i am looking for my soul mate...if he exists, i dont see myself settling for anything less than that.

Or, how about this, from the dating Web site for Jewish singles:

PICKY PROFILE #3

WOMAN LOOKING FOR, WELL, UTTER PERFECTION

I was instant messaging my mother tonight and I told her that I was in the process of re-joining jdate. This was her response: "Change your profile on J-date to 'really &$%#&* up Jewish woman looking for the impossible because no man will ever do, but if you're out there, call me.'"

Ha! You've got to love these girls: they know what they want and they're not afraid to ask for it, but notice how, unlike Crocodile Chris, they see the irony and the humor in their reach-for-the-stars requests. Anyway, these ads got us thinking that maybe it's not so strange to eliminate guys from our PGHM lists just because we don't like their shoes. Or because they chew funny . . . or sing off-key . . . or think Hooters is fine dining.

John Tierney of *The New York Times* notices the trend and even has a name for it. He calls our generation's fault detector the "Flaw-O-Meter." He says it is that "inner voice, a little whirring device inside the brain, that instantly spots a fatal flaw in any potential mate." He coined the term after watching an episode of the TV show *Love Connection,* in which a guy disses a girl for having "dirty elbows." Dirty elbows? After surveying some friends and acquaintances, we're not in the least surprised by elbow discrimination.

Our random and not-very-scientific survey reveals that daters today would custom-order the DNA of their mates if they could (in fact, you'll read more about a DNA dating service later in this book). Check out the results of our informal look at the state of pickiness in twenty-first-century dating:

PICKY AND PICKIER:

ARE THESE GOOD REASONS TO REJECT A POTENTIAL MATE?

1. He has bad grammar (Ann, a university professor).
2. Her head is too big for her body (Jim, an eighty-year-old widower).
3. During dinner, he picked his teeth with the corner of the chopsticks wrapper (Doryne, daughter of eighty-year-old Jim).

(continued)

4. He doesn't believe in wearing belts (Doryne, again—she married the beltless guy and taught him to put on a belt).

5. He has "Billy Don't Be a Hero" and "King-Fu Fighting" on his iPod (Maggie, mother of three and community activist).

6. She has ugly toes (Mauricio, owner of a sports marketing business).

7. He has a gun collection—well, several gun collections—and he was packing when we went to the movies (Patty, president of a family-owned business).

8. He's never heard of *A Tree Grows in Brooklyn* (Roz, the daughter of Holocaust survivors).

9. He sells apple juice for a living (Roz again—if only she had realized she could have married someone who was in on the ground floor of Snapple!).

10. He was wearing tight designer jeans in a size smaller than mine (Bonnie, a writer).

11. He won't let me smoke in his house—in fact, he claims his entire Los Angeles neighborhood is a "nonsmoking canyon" and is off-limits (Ingrid, then a smoker, now a Pilates instructor).

12. He thinks the Olive Garden is fine dining (Maria, a lawyer).

13. He didn't know that Houston Street in Manhattan is pronounced "how-ston" not "hue-ston" (Joanne, Janice's pal).

14. He was wearing sweatpants with elastic ankles that made him look like Bill Cosby (Michelle, Janice's producer).
15. He put me in a cab after a date and didn't offer to pay for it (Erica, a fashion marketer).
16. He has a patch of hair in the middle of his back (Jeanine, a publicist).
17. Her purse is a mess (Janice's husband, Steve—believe us, it's still a mess).
18. His shoes are ugly (Janice).

Don't laugh or pass judgment. You know you have been there and probably still are because you are reading this book, right? Okay, we will let you slide a little. We're sure you'll agree that some of these dating deal-breakers are better than others. In fact, some of these reasons for nixing a potential date are actually worth heeding. The merit of each really depends on *you* and how much you are willing to bend. For example (we will buy this one), why should a professor settle for someone who doesn't know a misplaced subjunctive clause when he sees one? But the big head for the body, especially coming from an eighty-year-old? Come on.

Choosing a man because of his shoes is being picky. The dirty pocketbook? Too picky. And the big head, the ugly toes, and beltlessness? Picky, picky, and picky.

The New York Times's John Tierney points out that Manhattan and one of the smaller Hawaiian islands have the largest percentages of single households in the nation. We asked Dr. Laurie

PERSONAL SHOPPER TIP: Don't let the petty details be a dating deal-breaker. You're way too smart for that!

Weber, a psychologist who has treated plenty of picky New York singles, why consumer pickiness has spread with viral speed to relationships. Dr. Weber says, "People make a million excuses to cover up negative feelings about relationships. In my opinion, it all goes back to the family dynamic in which you grew up. If relationships feel like a burden to you, or if you associate loss or pain with relationships, you'll come up with lots of reasons to avoid being in a relationship. And think about it—we are a generation that has grown up with divorce like no other generation has."

In other words, it's all about fear. Being picky is just a way to appear discerning and selective when you're really just plain old scared. This makes sense to us, because most of the women we know who are super-picky never see themselves that way and in fact get angry if you suggest they are.

So, don't blame men if they are commitment phobes . . . we women are right there with them, ladies. Laura Berman, Ph.D., author of *The Passion Prescription*, a noted sex expert, and *Today Show* contributor, says being too picky is a way to avoid closeness. Later in this book, we'll talk more about resolving those underlying bad feelings you may have about yourself, or about relationships in general, but in the meantime, ask yourself: would you ever, ever, ever

Janice Says:

How many people would tell me that I was too picky? And how offended would I be? My first thought back then was that they don't have to sleep with the guy for the rest of their lives. But the pickier I got, the less my friends commented, and the sooner the blind dates started to dry up. No one wants to set you up with someone only to think it's a waste of a date. My friend Doryne (who, as you know, has her own pickiness issues) reminds me of how I passed on a nice guy because I didn't like the way he ate his yogurt. Oy ... did I have to grow up!

buy a bathing suit if you were super picky? No. So, think of a guy as a bathing suit, and get ready to make a purchase.

HERE'S HOW TO SCORE ON THE MEET MARKET

Don't fall prey to the pickiness epidemic—or you may never purchase a guy.

Rule #2:
Trade In Being Picky for Being Choosy

If you're being honest with yourself and think you might be suffering with the disease of our times—a pickiness problem—don't despair. There are plenty of others like you. In fact, it's a shopping style and it can be retrained. Step into our office.

PERSONAL SHOPPER TIP: It's never too late to learn to husband shop like a pro. Just learn how to manipulate the meet market to your advantage!

Let's look at how you behave in the mall. Are you taken in by labels and luster? Are you someone who tries on dress after dress, only to decide you really don't know what you're looking for after all? Or are you what we call a choosy shopper, someone who seeks style, satisfaction, and—above all else—value? In our opinion, it's okay to be choosy, but not crazily, insanely picky. Choosy means selectivity that is rational. Choosy means substance over style. In our opinion, choosy is good and picky is bad.

An honest self-assessment is half the battle, so ask yourself the following:

WHAT KIND OF SHOPPER AM I?

Persnickety and Picky	Chic and Choosy
• Packaging is all	• I look for performance and value
• Bergdorf's all the way	• I can find Marc Jacobs at Marshall's
• I pay full price	• I love a good sale
• I like to shop around, and shop, and shop . . .	• I know just what I'm looking for
• I believe I'll know it when I see it	• I shop with a list . . . and stick to it
• I love to shop all the time	• I've got better things to do
• I return . . . a lot	• I decide and get on with my life

Picky shoppers love trends, they love the latest, and they love the really expensive. And although those custom-made, designer-packaged, trendy items that picky shoppers love to bring home are fun once in a while, they have a not-so-hidden, megabucks price tag. Most of the time they don't deliver that extra oomph we were hoping for . . . it's just a temporary "high," like the one you get after eating a piece of good chocolate cake.

Yes, sometimes, designer price tags result from fine tailoring, quality materials, and museum-quality style. But just as often—maybe more often?—they are directly related to huge advertising budgets, Madison Avenue rents, and hype.

The same goes for shopping for guys. Girls (and shoppers in general) who are choosy—and not crazy picky—know these rules:

HOW TO BE CHOOSY

1. Don't Fall for Extravagant Packaging: Tiffany's trademark blue box, Hermès's orange one, the red soles of a Christian Louboutin shoe. We know the signifiers of high style and we'll pay for them. And pay, and pay, and pay. It's like meeting that fabulous guy, you know, the investment banker or surgeon who lives in Buckhead or Pacific Heights, only to find out later on that he would rather go on a date with his mother instead of you. Don't ask . . . we're sure you've been there. These extravagantly packaged guys will sometimes put you into sticker shock with their great credentials and fancy résumés. They'll wine and dine you, take you on luxury vacations, but just as often, they won't deliver when it comes to the "C" word. Yes, we'll say it: commitment. It's not a dirty word.

2. Don't Fall in Love with the Fancy Retail Experience: According to *Vogue* magazine and the Luxury Institute,

Bergdorf Goodman is considered to be the United State's most prestigious luxury department store. No surprise there, with its address at the crossroads of Fifth Avenue and 59th Street, near the Plaza Hotel, and at the foot of Central Park. Shoppers associate luxury with high-rent districts and are willing to pay accordingly. They may be disappointed later, though, to see the same goods for a cheaper price at a strip mall on the side of the interstate, way outside of town. Don't fall for that great Mr. Big apartment or that fabulous car. That alone won't cut it.

3. Don't Have a Romance with the Price Itself: As Marvin Traub, a retail consultant in New York, points out to *The New York Times,* "Price itself is part of the status of certain luxury items." Price is not always directly related to value. A high price can add cachet, a certain je ne sais quoi, a frisson of excitement and exclusivity that can turn a day of shopping into something special. Just don't ask how you'll feel once the shopper's high subsides. We all know the type of guy who is all flash and no substance. His appeal is in his price. He's so hot you can't believe it . . . or his powerful job is an aphrodisiac. Once you get him—especially if you can't believe he picked you—it's hard to let him go. But if he doesn't deliver, let him go. After all, what do you wear more? The great-fitting white Gap T-shirt or that Hermès scarf you received from one of your castoffs?

Choosy shoppers know that the "designer guy," the one with the nice toes and the good music on his iPod, may not be worth what you'll pay for him. If you're so picky that you're holding out for a sensitive, French-speaking, New-Orleans-jazz-loving, Ivy-League-educated, squash-playing, Hugo Boss–clad cancer researcher with no children, no ex-wives, a full head of hair, and a paid-off mortgage, you may be missing the point. The designer guy may cost you in time and trouble—and even more likely, you may never find him. In the meantime, you may have overlooked the essentials and a perfectly good buy on a guy.

Now, we're not here to tell you to give up and grab the next shlub who messages you online. As we'll discuss later, selectivity can be a quality that men actually find very attractive. But we are here to tell you to be choosy or selective and not picky, and the following rules will show you how to do just that.

HERE'S HOW TO SCORE ON THE MEET MARKET

Become a *choosy* shopper—and leave those overpriced designer guys in the dressing room.

Janice's Wedding

"Uncompromising," "exacting." These are the words *The New York Times* used to describe my husband, Steve, in the "Vows" column that announced our engagement. A friend described Steve as someone who was looking for a "Martha Stewart type" who would also share his deep spirituality. Pretty picky? You could say that I had met my match.

I guess I have no right to laugh at him (although I do). When the talented actor, journalist, and talk show host Charles Grodin found out I wasn't married, he started a campaign on his CNBC talk show to find a guy for me. Not a bad offer, huh? He asked me what I was looking for. "Smart, good-looking, wealthy, athletic, with a sense of humor," I quickly reeled off. Every few weeks, Grodin would bring me back on his show and ask for an update on my dating life. I had lots of dates. But never a winner.

As fate would have it, Steve's father saw me on Grodin's show and told Steve to call me. "She looks like a nice girl," he told Steve. "You should call her." Steve just laughed and said, "Dad, she'll think I'm a stalker." And so he never called.

Despite Charles Grodin's (and my own) efforts, I couldn't find Mr. Right. On the last segment in which I appeared, Grodin gave me some advice I'll never forget. As *The New York Times* explained:

> *The gambit was meant as a joke, but in the final segment Mr. Grodin . . . turned sincere. Perhaps, he suggested, Ms. Lieberman was looking for the wrong five things and suggested five more. "You want somebody who loves you, cares about your family, somebody you can trust, who's kind and who wants children," he told her.*

(continued)

Charles Grodin was right. Steve and I met years later at a class on a topic that interested us both: spirituality. As I told *The New York Times*, with Steve, I got all ten qualities, the ones I was looking for, and the ones Charles Grodin taught me really count.

Grodin knew something I didn't know at the time. I was being picky instead of being choosy. I was looking for the stuff that may matter in the short run, but not in the long run. So was Steve. Luckily, by the time we finally met, we were ready to get serious. At that point, we had both learned to be selective, not picky.

Any "olympic shopper" knows the real truth: in marriage-shopping, look for the long-distance run. Don't think only about what you want today (or tonight). Think about what you will want twenty, thirty, even fifty years down the road. Looks and athletics may be long gone by then, but trust, caring, and family values don't slip away with time.

Rule #3:
Don't Settle When You Shop . . . But Be Willing to Compromise

Now it's *almost* time to start your very own PGHM shopping list, right after this one last cautionary story:

Writer Lori Gottlieb knows from pickiness. She spent her twenties and thirties writing off men who were admittedly PGHM because she was searching for that extra something. Like so many of us, though, she wasn't sure exactly what that something was—but she was sure she'd know it when she saw it. Now in her forties, having never found that designer guy she was searching for, she recently wrote an article for *The Atlantic* that touched a nerve and landed her on *The Today Show* because of the radical proposition she made to the women of America.

> *My advice is this: Settle. That's right. Don't worry about passion or intense connection. Don't nix a guy based on his annoying habit of yelling "Bravo" in movie theaters. Overlook his*

halitosis or abysmal sense of aesthetics. Because if you want to have the infrastructure in place to have a family, settling is the way to go.

Yes, Gottlieb went ahead and she said it. It's the "S" word, the word that is anathema to single women everywhere. No one, no matter how badly she wants to get married, ever, *ever* wants to "settle."

Is settling inevitable, though? Our mothers told us "there are plenty of fish in the sea." Were they wrong? As United States universities pump out graduates on a 60 percent female 40 percent male ratio, and as our cities fill with what seems like a surplus of talented, beautiful, well-educated women, are we all heading for a rude awakening in which settling will simply be the name of the game?

Yikes, even in the animal kingdom, settling seems to be a necessity. Check out this Cornell University professor's description of what goes down in the monkey world:

THE ANIMAL KINGDOM:
THEY SETTLE! WHO KNEW?

Perhaps there is a fundamental rule of mating that is clear to primates. Given the opportunity, any female would choose the best possible mate over a loser. But the pool out there is not exactly full of great possibilities, so a female must make do. At the very least she should make sure her reproductive tract is full of sperm when conception is likely. In most cases, female choice probably takes a backseat to the stronger urge to conceive when the time is right. And so female choice may end up being more of a compromise than a real choice.

—Meredith F. Small, Ph.D.,
professor of anthropology, Cornell University

Uh-oh. If even monkeys are settling, does this mean that we humans had better get real, too? Is settling a fact of life?

Well, most women would certainly rather believe that it is not. Settling, in our minds, means selling ourselves short. It means giving up the dream, it means resigning to fate—it's just not the American way. We, the people, or at least the women of America, hate the idea of settling. It's a betrayal of that finely honed sense of taste and individuality (also known as pickiness) to which we are all so very attached.

Okay, we know. You're now expecting us to tell you that you'll have to settle, that settling is sensible and realistic and the only way to go.

Wrong.

We don't want you to settle any more than you want to settle. *No settling allowed!* After all, as one blogger put it in response to Gottlieb's article:

Look at the flip side. Do you want a man to ask you to marry him because he's decided to settle for you? Because you'll do in a pinch? Because you're Miss Good Enough? Do you want to live your life married to a man who was never really thrilled to have you as his own? Not me! So why would I do that to some nice man?

Dr. Dale Atkins, Ph.D., the psychologist and relationship expert who has appeared many times on *The Today Show*, agrees. She says, "No one wants to feel that you settled for them and they are not good enough. You have to give up the fantasy of what he isn't and accept who he is and embrace it." Laura Berman, M.D., sex expert, professor at Northwestern University School of Medicine, and a *Today Show* contributor, agrees: "I don't believe in settling." Dr. Berman says that if you feel you're settling, you probably don't have the sexual chemistry that, according to her, is essential in a good marriage.

We say, "Amen!" Settling, if it really feels like settling, is a nonstarter. You should never go into a marriage thinking you did what you "should" do, but not want you "want" to do.

But what *we* want you to do is to learn to be selective, like a good consumer, and to understand this will entail some compromising.

That's right: you have to learn to compromise.

PERSONAL SHOPPER TIP: Never settle for less than great, but you can compromise on the price you are willing to pay. A little bartering can get you a great buy!

So, what is the difference between settling and compromising? Compromising means you may have to make a paradigm shift. It may mean you need to look at your old criteria for guys—you know, the "no Wrangler jeans" and "no rotisserie baseball"—and replace it with new criteria. That's not settling.

That's compromising, and compromising is never wrong. Well, almost never.

Dr. Laurie Weber, the New York City psychologist, explains it this way: "You won't think of it as settling if you're really open to a relationship and realistic about what a relationship entails. The reality is that love means compromise. A relationship that is successful is an acceptance of another human being in their entirety—as a whole."

If you're not sure you understand the difference between compromising and settling, study the following:

DON'T SETTLE—COMPROMISE!
OR . . . TO DUMP OR NOT TO DUMP, THAT IS THE QUESTION

SETTLING: I'm not sexually attracted to him, but I guess he's a good provider, so what the heck. (*Dump Him!*)

COMPROMISING: I've had hotter sex in my life, but he really wants to make me happy . . . and he's awfully cute. (*Keep Him!*)

SETTLING: When he gets mad I have to leave his apartment because he's kinda scary, but he really can't help it because his dad was abusive, ya know? (*Dump Him!*)

COMPROMISING: He pronounces Van Gogh like Van Go instead of Van Gok and my coworkers at the gallery snicker behind his back. Frankly, I get a little embarrassed for him. (*Keep Him!*)

SETTLING: He has a tiny problem with alcohol, but only

(continued)

when he's on deadline and c'mon—all great artists are troubled and need to self-medicate, don't they? (*Dump Him!*)

COMPROMISING: He travels a lot—I mean a *lot*—for his job, but so do all of President Obama's foreign policy advisors, right? (*Keep Him!*)

SETTLING: He doesn't really like any of my friends, but I understand—my friends are really shallow and silly sometimes and he's so deep and brilliant that I don't even understand him half the time. (*Dump Him!*)

COMPROMISING: So, he wants to go on an annual trip with his ten best buddies—he has a lot of friends from college. (*Keep Him!*)

Settling leaves you feeling gypped, and it is no way to start a marriage. Believe us, if you feel like you caved on Day One, you will feel *really* miserable if you even make it to Day Three Hundred and Sixty-five. Compromising, on the other hand, leaves you feeling like you got a good deal: it means you understand that no one is perfect (including yourself), and that although you got all the important stuff in your mate (which we will outline in the next few rules), you understand you'll have to let some of the bells and whistles slide. As Dr. Dale Atkins says, "You can't have it all. No one is perfect. You have to realize that." In other words, compromise is key.

Dr. Atkins speaks from experience. When she was first introduced to her future husband, he was "everything I thought I didn't want." Too old, too Wall Street, too many kids—this would have been the litany of complaints had she heard about Rob before she met him. But as soon as she did meet him, Dr. Atkins says, "I knew I would marry my husband after we had lunch the first time. I absolutely knew." The moral of the story? Compromise can be painless with the right guy.

MEREDITH VIEIRA:
ACCEPTING THE GOOD, THE BAD, AND THE SOMETIMES JERKY

When Meredith Vieira, the *Today Show*'s wonderful co-anchor, recounts how she met and married her husband, it sounds a little like *Woman of the Year*, that great old Katharine Hepburn–Spencer Tracy movie about two reporters whose initial irritation at each other and competitive sparring jump-start a true love story.

Meredith was a young reporter in Chicago covering late-night fires and car crashes when she first met her husband-to-be, Richard Cohen. He walked into the television station where Meredith was curled up on a couch, resting between assignments. "I was watching Bugs Bunny under a blanket when this hot-shot New York producer working with Leslie Stahl came in to do a big story on the governor." According to Meredith, he had a sarcastic, know-it-all attitude, and he invited her to "watch him" edit his story. Then he asked her what she thought of it. "I said, 'I thought you missed the point.' I knew I was going to marry him, even though I thought he was kind of a jerk," Meredith says.

(continued)

They met again in New York after Meredith had become a national correspondent. "He took me to a seedy bar for a drink. I thought, 'Wow, he's really cheap.'" As Katharine Hepburn would surely agree, sometimes the frisson of competition and a little button pushing can make a girl overlook a problem or two. But Meredith's star was rising and her bosses and colleagues wondered whether marriage would get in the way of her career.

"Most women who work in this business are read the riot act: 'You can get married but we may not be able to keep you. You need to be on call all the time.' Then you wake up and say, 'What did I do with my life?' I didn't want to end up watching tapes of myself, all alone, as I got older. After all, it's not all about your job. Your job is not who you are—it's just a part of who you are," Meredith says.

Meredith was not going to let her job keep her from personal happiness. "I knew I wanted kids and I wanted to be married to have them." If that is your goal, too, Meredith says, "Don't get caught up with stupid things. Don't put up walls that you don't even realize you are putting up. Sit down with a friend or therapist and say, 'Is there something you see that I'm doing?'"

Married almost twenty-five years now and the mother of three children, she knows she made the right decision: "The qualities I like about Richard are his sense of humor, that he is smart and strong, and that he values friendship and keeps old friends. He's also a great father."

Life, as always, provides plenty of challenges. Emmy award–winning Cohen was diagnosed at age twenty-five with multiple sclerosis. Meredith says, "He told me he had MS when we dated. I was sort of blasé about it. I felt he was better off than many others and it could have been worse. He is sixty now and needs a cane . . . so what? If I get mad I might kick the cane—not because of the MS but because he might be acting like a jerk!"

Some things never change.

So, think of a guy as a car: make sure you get a highly rated, safe vehicle with what you consider to be nice, sleek lines. But as far as the color of the interior—and maybe even the satellite radio—you may have to love it the way it comes (or install your own later).

HERE'S HOW TO SCORE ON THE MEET MARKET

We say don't settle, but be selective in what matters to you and what you are willing to compromise on. Look for the qualities that make a guy a good buy.

THE AGE DILEMMA

The reality is that the pool of eligible men does dwindle as the years pass. According to the U.S. Census Bureau, for every one hundred single women in their twenties, there are 120 single (never married, widowed, or divorced) men available. Ahh, youth. As one twenty-nine-year-old

(continued)

we know put it to us recently, "When you are in your twenties, you are what every guy wants. The younger guys want you, the older guys want you. It's great!" Unfortunately, things go south from there. For every one hundred single women over sixty-five, there are only thirty-four—that's right, thirty-four—single men. This doesn't mean that the statistics quoted by that old *Newsweek* article are true—you know, the one that said women over forty had a 2 percent chance of ever getting married? That article has long been discredited, with *Newsweek* itself now saying that forty-year-olds have a "40 percent if not better" chance of marrying. But no one would disagree that the pool of marriageable men is inversely related to age. In other words, the older we get, the fewer good men there are out there.

The truth is that the time to be picky is when you are twenty, twenty-five, maybe thirty. As the years pass, it's time to be choosy and to learn to compromise. Sorry, ladies, but over thirty, your picky days should be over.

Rule #4:
Choosy Shoppers Choose . . .
a Guy with Good Guts

So, what are the qualities that make a guy a good buy? What are the characteristics that are *not* worth compromising? And what should go on your PGHM shopping list?

Maureen Dowd cited in her *New York Times* column not long ago the words of Father Pat O'Connor, a Catholic priest who lectures teenage girls on how to find the ideal husband. His advice was so startlingly simple, it caused people to talk. "Never marry a man who has no friends," Father O'Connor advises, because they will be "incapable of the intimacy that marriage demands." So true. And why do his words come as a surprise? Because we don't think about the plain-and-simple—we choose to believe that life is so much more complicated than that.

Let's start with the basics. These are the core values—the ones that civilized cultures generally agree make someone a good husband, a righteous person, and an upstanding member of society. These values are like the wiring in a house, the engine of a car, the cut and clarity of a diamond ring. They're the fundamentals, the basics, the mechanics . . . and they simply cannot be compromised. We call them the "guts" of a guy and we recommend shopping first and foremost for this: a "guy with good guts."

In Christianity there are the seven holy virtues: chastity, temperance, charity, diligence, kindness, patience, and humility. Or, as Father O'Connor points out: a responsible attitude toward money, a sense of humor, and a supportive family. In Judaism, a good Jewish husband must respect parents and teachers, must never harm others, must not steal, be sexually unfaithful, use hurtful speech, or covet things owned by others. In Islam, according to the ancient scholar Ibn Qutayba, an ideal husband is generous, pious, kind, and courageous. In Buddhism, Sikhism— heck, all the isms—the idea is the same. A good catch is a person of integrity, honor . . . and someone who doesn't break the law.

You get the idea.

PERSONAL SHOPPER TIP: We say you should spend most of your shopping energy on searching for a guy with good guts because good guts always get a 10 on the PGHM Meter.

You may think it seems obvious, but imagine how much better off we'd all be if we heard "I'm looking for a respectful man who is honest and diligent" as often as we hear "I'm looking for a cute guy who likes to travel, go to the movies, and take long walks on the beach." You may not get a saint, but if you're seeking the core values in a mate, and they are foremost in your mind and at the top of your shopping list, you're more likely than not to get them (at least in their imperfect, human form). As Dr. Atkins puts it: "What is most important is how they treat women and how they talk about other people. Is he nice to the waitress . . . is he nice to his own family? You have to see what a person is made of." That's good guts.

Like good mechanics in a car or sound structure in a house, good guts are not flashy and often can't even be seen from the outside. They take a bit of inspection to uncover. Sometimes, we may even need an expert to come in and tell us that the basics are in order. That's when a trusted and wise friend (not your jealous roommate from college), an impartial relative (impartial being key, see Part II, Rule #8), or even a spiritual advisor can weigh in and give you their opinion. Later on, we'll talk about how to do your research when "buying" a man, but for now, suffice it to say that the core values are the most important factors you should be looking for when buying a guy. Assure yourself that everything with respect to these values is in order.

Please don't think we're trying to tell you that you can't settle for anything less than a saintly rabbi who can recite the Koran with Zenlike reserve. What we're really telling you is to strike from your list anyone who is disloyal, lazy, unethical, unkind, disrespectful, or just plain mean. In our old life we thought those qualities were "cute" or "sexy." Seriously, ladies, grow up. We know you know good guts when you see it. Listen to your own gut (it's just about always right), go while the going is good, and make the cut. Don't tell yourself stories, don't live in a fantasy world, and don't waste your time on nogoodniks. You can compromise (not

GOOD GUTS IN A GUY: IS HE PERFECTLY GOOD HUSBAND MATERIAL?

He is a good friend (and actually has a few).

PGHM Meter: 10

He's kind to his mother (even if she's a bitch).

PGHM Meter: 10

He seems to like women (but not too much!).

PGHM Meter: 10

He doesn't have a record (as in arrest, not CD).

PGHM Meter: 10

He's polite to waiters (and to people who work for him).

PGHM Meter: 10

He likes animals (or at least doesn't hurt them).

PGHM Meter: 10

He is not heavily in debt (excluding student loans).

PGHM Meter: 10

He doesn't abuse drugs, alcohol, or people (period).

PGHM Meter: 10

He doesn't lie (at least not recreationally).

PGHM Meter: 10

He can keep a job (for six months or more).

PGHM Meter: 10

and

He is never, ever violent (as in *ever*).

PGHM Meter: 10+++++

settle) on a guy who hasn't read Proust, or who's losing his hair, or who grinds his teeth when he sleeps. But there's no settling allowed for a guy made from cheap materials.

PERSONAL SHOPPER TIP: Listen to your own gut in order to find a guy with good guts!

And if you don't know what to think, if you are uncertain or confused or getting mixed messages, get quiet, meditate, pray, or take a walk somewhere you can think. Then listen to what your very own gut tells you. And believe what you hear. Remember, a good friend or parent usually does want the best for you and will be willing to spill the honest truth . . . just don't get mad at them when they do.

HERE'S HOW TO SCORE ON THE MEET MARKET

Don't settle for less than a guy with good mechanics. Instead, make it a priority to look for good guts—core values in tip-top shape.

THE MAN'S PERSPECTIVE:
CHARLES GRODIN

Who knows more about, well, everything, than Charles Grodin? Think about it. The man has done it all: actor, political commentator, journalist, and talk show host. He also knows a thing or two about marriage, as I learned when he wisely counseled me through many single days.

We asked him, "What is the single most important

(continued)

thing to look for in a prospective spouse? What is the number one characteristic that girls should be looking for in a man?"

"I think it is crucial to find someone with a good disposition," he told us.

Grodin says that you rarely know how time will change a person, but one thing that stays the same over the years is a person's general disposition. So, pick a spouse, Grodin says, who is kind and pleasant. After all, looks and sexual appeal may all fade with time. "Sexy and good-looking is great, but you are best off if you can marry your best friend." A kind person, Grodin points out, is and remains a kind person.

Good advice from a man who seems to us to know it all, and Charles Grodin took his own advice: his delicious wife is kind, bright, and beautiful, both inside and out.

Rule #5:
Be Sure to Check Under the Hood and Buy a Model with a Powerful Engine

What's the engine of a marriage? Sex, duh! Yes, it's the little engine that could . . . keep a marriage going, that is. And how do you make sure you get a powerful engine? It's all in the laws of attraction. We're not talking The Secret. We're talking sex. So listen up.

Let's face it, ladies. Marriage is for the long haul, a good marriage anyway, and it's not easy to keep the sexual chemistry alive twenty, thirty, or fifty years down the road. So, if we want a marriage that lasts and lasts and doesn't conk out along the way, we need good sex—the "powerful engine" of a marriage.

According to Dr. Laura Berman, the sexologist, the seeds of attraction must exist at the early stages of a relationship. She says sexual technique can be learned or perfected later. She also says the sex you have doesn't have to be the most fabulous, outrageous,

PERSONAL SHOPPER TIP: When you are in the initial stages of a relationship, here's what you look for: *sexual attraction.* It has to be there from the get-go.

rock-your-world sex that you've ever had. This is important, so we'll say it again: it doesn't have to be rock-star, motorcycle sex! But there does have to be that initial attraction. Call it good old-fashioned chemistry.

What is chemistry, anyway, you may ask, and how do you find it? What makes a girl go weak in the knees (and everywhere else) for one guy and not another? Why is it that some guys who are perfectly nice—who you know are PGHM—just don't get you going?

Well, according to Dr. Berman, attraction is a chemical response, and it is connected to the hormone oxytocin—the same chemical that kicks in when you have an orgasm. And that stuff they say about pheromones, well, it may be true. Some guys—their smell, their hair color, their temperament—trigger all those fun hormones! We say, bring them on! But why do some guys float our boats, and how do we find more of them?

Dr. Berman is a believer in the "love map," a theory of attraction developed by the late John Money, Ph.D., a psychologist and sexologist who coined the term "gender role." Dr. Money said the template that we are attracted to—the type of guy, the color of hair, the build, the personality—is solidified by the time we are age seven. In Dr. Berman's words,

A love map is a product of early childhood experiences that lay the groundwork for our attractions after puberty. The information, like having a favorite babysitter when you were younger, registers in the brain via the five senses. You remember her hair color. Or you develop an affinity for her body type. Later, you're "activated" by these very same qualities. You walk into a crowded room and someone catches your eye. Or you feel the pangs of attraction when someone speaks like her. Love maps explain why we feel that certain pull toward someone without knowing why.

Dr. Berman said it is good to be sensitive to what your love map is, but you should remember one thing: it is an unconscious attraction, so you never know when it will be triggered. In other words, *be open!* What's ugly to others, according to Dr. Berman, could be delicious to you. Attraction may strike when you least expect it. But the bottom line is this: attraction must be there, or you should be off to the stores again!

HERE'S HOW TO SCORE ON THE MEET MARKET

Keep the engine of your relationship powered up and humming by basing it on attraction: sexual attraction, that is! Sexual Attraction is a PGHM Meter 10!

THE CASE FOR MARRIAGE?

Q: Why should I want to get married, anyway? This is 2009! Isn't marriage an antiquated relic? And with divorce rates at such high levels, isn't it a broken relic at that? Why, oh why, go through all of the pain?

(continued)

A: Fine. No one says you *have* to get married. Heck: Susan B. Anthony, Janet Reno, Joan of Arc, Maureen Dowd . . . not bad company to be in. And if marriage means obliterating your freedom and becoming totally dependent on a man—financially, emotionally, and every other way—we say, forget it. But marriage should mean sharing your life, for better and worse, and that's a wonderful thing. Besides, there is evidence that, as compared to unmarried women, married women are healthier, happier, live longer, and are financially better off. This is not to say that a bad marriage is better than no marriage. This is, in our opinion, most definitely *not* true! But a good marriage is a good thing.

Rule #6:
Look for a Garment—Oops, We Mean a Guy—Who Will Withstand the Test of Time: Seek out a Little Black Dress Among Men

If you consider good guts and a powerful engine to be the baseline—the line beneath which you will not, must not, settle—what else should be on your PGHM shopping list? Well, you want someone who will go the distance with you, "till death do you part." The problem is, how do you know who will be sitting across from you in a rocker on Delray Beach in 2050, tenderly holding your hand, and who will end up living with wife number four on Lexington Avenue along with your children's much younger half-siblings?

Fortunately for us, scientists have been working diligently, and not just to uncover the secrets of the human genome or discover the cure for cancer. They've been studying marriage, specifically addressing this essential question: what makes a marriage happy in the long run? And isn't that exactly what we need to know in order to narrow down our shopping list further?

After all, when you shop for a car, you look for cars that retain their value over the long haul. When you shop for a dress, you know that if it's a classic—a black cocktail dress with flattering lines, for example—you will be happy with it three, five, even ten years down the road. And in marriage, if we're really going to make it work we'd better know the following: what is Super Glue in the world of marriage and what is curling, yellowed Scotch Tape? And, as long as we're waxing metaphoric, who are the guys who make good hubbies in the long-distance marathon of a happy marriage, and who are the short-distance sprinters fit only for a fling? *Who are the "little black dresses" among men?*

PERSONAL SHOPPER TIP: Pick a guy who is a classic, a neutral, someone who will blend in with your entire wardrobe of friends and family—and leave the trendy fads in the store. You'll be happy you did.

You may not believe it, but according to cutting-edge scientific research, the guy who is willing to go the distance with you is a not-so-great-looking, dishwashing, mellow yet upbeat college grad who makes a very nice living. He doesn't go for the jugular in an argument, he likes sex but he's not a sex maniac, and he knows when to let you have your way (which is often). So, here's the scoop:

HOW TO SPOT A GUY WHO
IS A LITTLE BLACK DRESS:
WE DIDN'T MAKE IT UP—IT'S SCIENCE, OK?

He's uglier than you.	PGHM Meter: 7
He washes the dishes.	PGHM Meter: 9
He lets you have your way.	PGHM Meter: 8
He's college educated.	PGHM Meter: 7
He's not type A.	PGHM Meter: 8
He earns more money than you.	PGHM Meter: 6
He's not overly sexual.	PGHM Meter: 6
He's not isolated or super grumpy.	PGHM Meter: 9

Okay, let's discuss:

1. He's Uglier Than You. That's right. According to a study by UCLA's associate professor of social psychology, Benjamin R. Karney, Ph.D., reported in the *Journal of Family Psychology,* if you're hotter than he is, even just a little, you both will be more content in the long run. So, look for a guy who's a little less gifted than you are in the looks department.

Actually, it makes some sense to us. He'll be less likely to stray if he thinks he got the better end of the deal—and who wants to be the less cute one in the relationship, anyway? This rule also explains several social phenomena if you think about it: trophy wives, the younger replacement wife (what we call the secondary market). Aren't they just replacements that allow the desired balance of power (him: uglier; you: prettier) to remain intact? So, think ugly. Just a little. It'll be fine.

2. He Washes the Dishes. The Pew Research Center in Washington asked more than two thousand people what makes a happy marriage, and they found that sharing household chores was right up at the top of the list, just behind faithfulness and a good sex life. Of course it is— who wants to be the one doing all the chores alone for a lifetime? No, thank you. Listen to us: ten years down the road, willingness to vacuum after a party will trump the presence of washboard abs. And chances are, the washboard abs will be gone by then, anyway.

3. He Lets You Have Your Way. Researchers at Iowa State University looked at seventy-two couples and discovered that happy couples are the ones in which the woman's opinion rules on how to solve problems in the home or in the marriage. Amen. Sure, that macho decisiveness is nice for a month or so, but wouldn't you be happier if you got to pick the color of the living room walls? Of course you would. Admit it.

Janice Says...

Steve gives in to me all the time. He knows it's easier for him to have a lasting relationship, and in the end he usually thinks I am right. On occasion I will let him have it his way. We rarely fight because we think to ourselves: what is the alternative? Start shopping for a mate again? No thanks.

How to Shop for a Husband

Okay, do we hear you grinding your teeth? Are you thinking: who wants to marry a wimp? We're not talking wimp here. We're talking a confident guy who is busy enough with his own interests and his own business affairs and his own circle of friends that he doesn't have time to meddle in the part of your life you would happily control. So, if you like to dress yourself and think you've been doing it well enough without him, then we say, pick a guy who knows to keep his opinions to himself.

4. He's College Educated. Divorce rates are much lower among people with college degrees than those with less education. Nice to know that paper on "The Hegelian Dialectic as It Applies to the Napoleonic Wars" will finally pay off. Steven P. Martin, Ph.D., assistant professor of sociology at the University of Maryland, calls it "the divorce divide." He says, "From the 1970s to the 1990s, rates of marital dissolution fell by almost half among four-year college graduates, but remained relatively high and steady among women with less than a four-year college degree." Invest in education; it's good for you, especially if you want to stay married.

5. He's Not Type A. A high household income is a good predictor of a happy marriage, but a guy who is too tense, too driven, or too uptight will not make you happy— at least if that's how you perceive him to be. According to a study in the *Journal of Occupational Behaviour,* higher levels of perceived type-A behavior correlate with an unhappier spouse. So, he should be successful and

HOW LIKELY IS DIVORCE, ANYWAY?

Is it true that marriages today have a 50 percent chance of ending in divorce? The experts say no. Although it's more complicated than you would think to get an accurate assessment of the chances that a marriage will end in divorce, the overall rate is probably closer to 40 percent. Divorce rates have been falling in the United States since 1981, so for those of you who are children of the 1970s, you have a better chance of staying married than your parents did.

Analysis of divorce trends in America also reveals that if you fall into any of the following categories, your chance of divorce is *less* than the national average:

- Annual income over fifty thousand dollars
- Waited until after marriage to have a child
- College graduate
- Parents didn't divorce
- Some sort of religious affiliation
- Married after age twenty-five
- First marriage (second marriages have a higher divorce rate)

The reality is probably something like this: Your chances of divorce if you marry at twenty because you are pregnant and you never make it through college? Astronomically high. Your chances of divorce if you marry at thirty or older, are relatively affluent, and college educated? Not so bad. Not so bad at all.

driven, but not too. You are willing to let him work to make a buck, but still want him home to diaper the baby. Got it?

6. He Earns More Money Than You. We really hate to say this, because it goes against our you-go-girl mindsets, but here's the scoop: Steven L. Nock, Ph.D., director of the Marriage Matters Project at the University of Virginia says a wife is less likely to want to stay in the marriage—and is more likely to want to trade up—if she makes more money than her mate. Note we said wife, not husband—it's you who will want out, not him, if you bring home more of the bacon. The scientists say so; we didn't make it up. Okay, not very "PC," but that's what the research suggests.

Our own anecdotal research is split on this one. We do have friends who have opted out of the marriage once the women achieved domination in the budget department. Those annoying habits, those differing child-rearing theories, that lack of listening all became obvious and unbearable once splitting was no longer an insurmountable financial hardship. The sad part is how many women, even today in the 2000s, are stuck in yucky marriages because they are financially dependent.

On the other side of the spectrum, we know plenty of anchorwomen, correspondents, and businesswomen who happily make more money than a less "successful" hubby but are happy to do it because these guys are, in fact, great contributors to their marriages. They child-rear, work hard at less remunerative jobs, or are just lovely, supportive mates. So, as far as we're concerned, the jury's out on the salary wars issue.

7. He's Not Hyper-Sexual, Overly Kinky, or Surrounded by Hot Women at Work. The National Council on Family Relations reveals that guys with a huge libido, very permissive attitudes toward sex, and a lot of opportunity for philandering are at risk for straying. Think of every motorcycle-riding, rock-star-aspiring, hot, Brad-Pitt looka-like who has crossed your path and draw a circle around them with a diagonal line through it. They may be fun in the short run, but who needs the long-term trouble? Come on, ladies, we've all been there. Great hot nights that turn into cold mornings are a waste of a "hot" buy.

8. He's Not an Isolated, Grumpy, or Generally Unhappy Person. Sometimes those troubled troubadours, those lonely lotharios, and those soulful señors are just sooooo cute. You think it's your mission to cheer them up, but believe us, that's wasted energy, and it rarely works. Scientific studies say: *stay away*. Happier people have happier marriages. Laughing together is the aphrodisiac of all times. It's logical, it's proven, and so don't you forget it.

Just like a little black dress that looks great and retains its classic lines two, three, even five years down the road, the guy version of a little black dress is a keeper. Ten years from now, you'll be happy you chose a classic rather than a passing trend.

HERE'S HOW TO SCORE ON THE MEET MARKET

If you want a marriage that will withstand the test of time, then you want a guy who is a "little black dress." So think Jerry Seinfeld, not Brad Pitt; Bill Gates, not George Clooney. A little nebbishy, a little sensitive, a little homely: the studies say it's all good.

WHAT WOULD JANE SAY?
DATING ACCORDING TO JANE AUSTEN

I could not be happy with a man whose taste did not in every point coincide with my own. He must enter into all my feelings; the same books, the same music must charm us both. . . . Mama, the more I know of the world, the more am I convinced that I shall never see a man whom I can really love. I require so much.

—Marianne, *Sense and Sensibility*

Anything is to be preferred or endured rather than marrying without Affection; and if his deficiencies of Manner &c &c strike you more than all his good qualities, if you continue to think strongly of them, give him up at once. . . .

Wisdom is better than Wit, & in the long run will certainly have the laugh on her side.

—Letter from Jane Austen to her niece, Fanny Knight, about Mr. John Plumptre, whom Fanny was considering marrying, November 18, 1814

Rule #7:
Be Sure to Use the Mirror in the Dressing Room: Learn the Mirror-Image Rule

Nothing is worse than trying on a bathing suit in a well-lit dressing room that provides a 360-degree view of all your dimples and ripples. But when looking for a husband, it's essential to learn to use the mirror. Why? Only because numerous studies show that in marriage, we look for someone a lot like ourselves—and are happiest when we find our mirror image, or someone pretty close to it.

For some of us it's as natural as a reflex: we end up with a guy, and everyone tells us, "Hey, you kinda look like your boyfriend, you know?" We all know plenty of couples that look alike (or grow to look alike after several years). Maybe those mirror images become the "type" of guy we always seek out, and they can become a shopping pattern, in the same way we stick to one style of khaki pants or always end up leaving the beauty counter with the same color of lipstick. But in the romance department, science backs up our instincts—we are happier with spouses who are like ourselves. So, for some of us it's natural to look for a guy who reflects ourselves.

Here's another interesting wrinkle in the look-alike data. A psychologist at Durham University in England and colleagues in Poland have determined that women who have a good relationship with their dads are attracted to men who resemble their fathers (who, in turn, may resemble themselves). So, whether it's a search for one's twin or one's dad, it's documented that daters search for someone who looks like himself or herself when seeking a mate.

But it's not just looks that draw similar people together. Researchers at Rutgers University are studying what makes a happy marriage—they call it the National Marriage Project. They say, "The more similar people are in their values, backgrounds, and life goals, the more likely they are to have a successful marriage." Scientists at Cornell University agree. They found that in addition to looks, similar wealth and social status ensure a better marriage. Their advice is not to try to "trade up" but to find your mirror image in terms of social status. In their opinion, opposites don't attract.

PERSONAL SHOPPER TIP: Forget the old adage that opposites attract and look for common ground. If you find it, you'll be enjoying your purchase for years to come!

Marriages between opposites face their own set of challenges. As *The New York Times*'s Jane Brody wrote of her own marriage between a reticent Midwesterner and a more voluble Russian-Jewish New Yorker: "While open communication is essential to the success of any close relationship, 'mixed' couples especially need to be certain that their messages are not only spoken and heard but understood and dealt with." As Brody points out, similar couples usually start off with a baseline of assumptions, understandings, and styles of communication. So, marriages between opposites can be an uphill battle and, as Brody says, "Love does not always conquer all."

Looks and similar backgrounds, though, are not the only bases of similarity upon which couples can converge. Studies spanning the past twenty-five years show that any of the following similarities can draw a couple together and help a relationship function well:

THE SIMILARITY RULE:
FIND YOUR MIRROR IMAGE

You and Your Guy—Do You Match on the Following:

Similar intelligence levels	PGHM Meter: 8
Similar emotional responses	PGHM Meter: 9
Similar personalities	PGHM Meter: 8

In fact, the science of similarities—*personality similarities*—is the secret behind eHarmony's matchmaking process. As Neil Clark Warren, Ph.D., the founder of eHarmony.com told *The Atlantic*, "In successful relationships, similarities are like money in the bank. Differences are like debts you owe. It's all right to have a few differences, as long as you have plenty of equity in your account." When you try to join eHarmony—and as the commercials for competing services point out, they may not accept you—you fill out an extensive online questionnaire that asks you to describe everything from the relative length of your fingers to the kinds of activities you enjoy. But eHarmony's matchmaking model is really based on this scientific premise: "Similarity in partners' personalities . . . increases the likelihood that they will have similar emotional experiences in their conversations, which in turn promotes more fulfilling relationships." In other words, the more alike you are, the more likely you'll be a match that works.

But what kind of similarities are we really talking about? The eHarmony Labs, which are associated with professors from the University of California, Los Angeles's Department of Psychology, tested in a sponsored study what psychologists call the Big Five Inventory (BFI). To put it simply, these are the five personality traits upon which you and your husband-to-be should agree (at least as much as possible) to predict what eHarmony hopes will be a long and happy life together.

Drum roll, please:

YOUR MIRROR IMAGE IN PERSONALITY:
WHAT TO LOOK FOR

1. *Extraversion.* Do you like to be around others, are you socially gregarious, could you be out every night? If so, so should he.

(continued)

2. *Agreeableness.* Do you see the cup as half full or half empty, are you cooperative or suspicious, do you play well with others? Make sure he does, too.

3. *Conscientiousness.* How responsible are you, do you take care of business, or are you likely to take a laissez-faire approach? A slacker and an Anal Annabel is a match made in hell.

4. *Neuroticism.* Woody Allen or not? This is a tendency to experience unpleasant personality traits such as anger, depression, or anxiety. Woody wrote a paean to Annie Hall for a reason.

5. *Openness to Experience.* Daredevil or dare-don't? You'd better both be on the roller coaster together . . . or not.

All of the Above—PGHM Meter: 8

We know the above is an oversimplification, but if the experts are using a more complicated version of this inventory as their methodology to match us up, why not try to use a simple version of it yourself? Try thinking about it in terms of yourself and your prospective other. You don't have to be photocopies of each other, but are you roughly similar in the Big Five categories or not?

At this point you may be asking yourself the following questions. Looks, age, background, personality: isn't similarity in all of these categories too much to ask for? And kinda boring, to boot? And what about opposites attracting? Seal and Heidi Klum look pretty good together. As do Ashton and Demi, and so many others.

The bottom line is this: you don't have to converge on all points to be similar enough to succeed as a couple. Heidi and Seal might come from different backgrounds and look different, but their Big Five might be in complete agreement. Ashton and Demi, while not the same age, are of similar attractiveness and may very well have precisely the same values and goals. Who knows? So try to rack up points of similarity, either in the looks department, or in family and cultural background, or in personality characteristics, or in all of the above. And yes, the more you two resemble one another in any and all, the better shot you'll have at making it, happily and easily, to your silver anniversary.

So, what goes on your PGHM shopping list? A description of yourself.

HERE'S HOW TO SCORE ON THE MEET MARKET

Check the mirror on the dressing room wall and repeat after us: "Mirror, mirror on the wall, find me a guy who looks and acts just like . . . me."

Rule #8:
Search for GUI:
Good User Interface

Ask the IT geeks in your office. The computer revolution would have gone nowhere without what they call GUI (pronounced "gooey"): graphical user interface. It's the part of your computer that you relate to—the icons, the desktop arrangement, and the overall look of the computer screen. It's how we humans can connect and communicate with computers, and it's the key that allows us to use the incredible technology at our fingertips. A computer with good GUI is a pleasure to work with, and makes our jobs so much easier.

Yup, you got it. Same with guys. When making your shopping list, be sure to look for good user interface, the kind of guy who communicates well, one who you can work things out with, one who fights fair.

Good communication. It's such a cliché that it has almost lost its meaning, but, interestingly, it *does* have a very specific meaning to the experts that is worth examining.

PERSONAL SHOPPER TIP: The killer app when it comes to guys is good communication.

Dozens upon dozens of studies show that two essentials—*really, truly hearing each other* and *fighting fair*—can make a dream relationship really last. The key is not to avoid conflict—that'll make you sick and miserable. The key is to communicate and especially to fight well. But what exactly does "good communication" mean? It means you gotta give and take, speak and be heard. So, here's the guy you're looking for: when you have a disagreement, he doesn't verbally abuse you, he listens, he tries to defuse, he doesn't dominate, and he even has a sense of humor. After speaking your truth, you will get the feeling that he heard what you had to say.

You both also need to know when to stop communicating. It's like deciding about a new dress. Sometimes you have to just buy it already. Remember that you don't have to "talk" about everything all the time. Know when it's time to let it go . . . or just buy that dress without further deliberation.

So, what have we learned so far? Good communication is more than a cliché and it had better be a reality in your relationship.

PERSONAL SHOPPER TIP: Communication sometimes means knowing when to say . . . nothing.

WHAT MAKES A GUY HAVE GOOD GUI?

He listens.	**PGHM Meter: 9**
He doesn't always dominate.	**PGHM Meter: 9**
He has a sense of humor—even when times are tense.	**PGHM Meter: 9**
He tries to diffuse arguments.	**PGHM Meter: 8**
He considers your point of view.	**PGHM Meter: 9**
He knows when enough is enough.	**PGHM Meter: 9**

HERE'S HOW TO SCORE ON THE MEET MARKET

It's all in the interface, so pick a good communicator.

Rule #9:
Listen to the *Real* Experts When Deciding on the Options

Let's take a moment to sum up our PGHM shopping list so far. We're looking for a guy with good guts. We want a relationship with a powerful engine. We are also seeking a keeper: someone who is a little black dress among men. Finally, we'd prefer someone who is like ourselves (the mirror image rule) and who has good GUI because he knows how to communicate well. Consider these the essentials.

Now it's time for the "options." There are plenty of good, solid cars out there and good, solid guys (really, once you start looking for substance and not style, they *are* out there). But how do we know what options to try for? Think leather seats, satellite radio, color of the trim—or, in guy terms, a love of music, a fantabulous job, a nice set of washboard abs. *Which bells and whistles do the good husbands have—the husbands who last and who are worth keeping—and which extras are not worth the money you pay for them?*

Well, we've already consulted the scientists to see if their double-blind, peer-reviewed, statistically sound studies can help us in the wild world of dating. As the last rule revealed, they can be helpful as far as the basics go. But when it comes to the extras—the options—science is not too helpful. Although the advent of computer dating has, for the first time in history, produced a wealth of quantifiable dating data, the science of romance and marriage is still in its infancy. So what's a girl to do?

Well, there's nothing like talking to the *real* pros. According to a study at the University of California, Berkeley, couples that are married a long time are better able to assess the likelihood of a marriage's success than are marital researchers. In three minutes, a group of long-married couples had a higher rate of success in telling which newlywed pairs would be married longest than did the shrinks.

In order to help you be the best husband consumer you can be, we assembled a group of long-married friends and acquaintances, in particular those who others have described as happily married, and we asked them what characteristics in their own husbands have been essential to the longevity of their marriages. In other words, what else should be on your shopping list? After all, if you are buying a car, a dishwasher, or a house in a new neighborhood, you ask others who have owned a similar product to see what they have to say. So we went to some successfully married couples and asked them the secrets of staying happily married.

The results may be surprising. Once you are happy with yourself and find someone who has good guts, good GUI, is a little black dress, and sufficiently satisfies the mirror-image rule,

PERSONAL SHOPPER TIP: When shopping for a big purchase—like a husband—consult those who really know the market. Your best bet: talk to the long and successfully married.

it doesn't really take all that much to make a happy marriage. A lot of options—good taste in music, being well read, appreciating fine wines—apparently aren't all that important. According to our girlfriends, it comes down to knowing yourself and knowing what you, personally, will find essential.

Here's what they had to say:

FOOD

"Once going to clubs and picking up cute guys and drinking too many Cosmos is a thing of the past, which it is pretty soon after you get married, what will you have left? You'll be able to go out to dinner. And if you like to eat, pick someone who likes to eat, too. He doesn't need to like exactly the same things you do. But generally, he should." That's according to Debbie, a retired law professor, who names a common interest in food as the single number one most important option you should be looking for in a guy. She should know—she's been married for more than twenty years. Debbie says if you are a fine diner, you'd better find someone who likes to dine accordingly. Vice versa for you fast-foodies. And if you're simply not interested in eating (Is there such a girl? If so, we don't know her), find your guy counterpart. *Similar taste in food: PGHM Meter: 8*

EDUCATION

It may be the final frontier. If there is one taboo that can't be crossed, one last dating deal-breaker, it may be education, at least according to Elizabeth, a New York publishing exec. Call it educationism if you must, but our experts agree that you and your husband should match, educationally speaking. Now, we're not going to be sticklers on this one and expect you to go master's degree for master's degree, or juris doctorate for, well, you get it. And as one twenty-something PR maven pointed out to us, some guys who haven't gone to college can make it up by being really well traveled, or super well read, or just perversely brilliant. But we have to agree that a strong disparity in educational level can't be good in the long run. *Similar education levels: PGHM Meter: 8*

SPORTS

If you are one of the, well, not rare, but minority of women to whom sports is an essential part of life, you'd better pick a guy who enjoys them as well. And why shouldn't you? There are plenty of those guys out there. But if you hate sports and he loves them? It's OK—let him hang out with his friends and bond. More time for you to do what you enjoy. So, get a life and let him have one too. *Shared love of sports: PGHM Meter: 5*

TELEVISION

Ahhh . . . America's favorite sport: watching TV. You love it, just admit it. And wouldn't it be nice—although we must say it's not essential—to have a list of TiVo faves that you can enjoy with your significant other? Sure it would, and the beauty of it all is that the same program can appeal to each of you for different reasons. Jeanine, a publicist, watches *The Hills* with her hubby: he likes to make fun of Spencer and the boys, and Jeanine likes to see what LC is wearing. Ingrid, a Pilates instructor, says that one of her best memories of married life involve a marathon weekend of watching *The Sopranos* in bed with her husband. Trading off also seems to be key when it comes to happily married TV viewing: you watch his if he'll watch yours. Anyone willing to trade an hour of the Yankees for an episode of *Project Runway*? Sounds like a deal to us! But some multiple TV households are also perfectly happy. Erica says: "I really wouldn't want to be married to a guy who's into the Kardashians or likes to watch *America's Next Top Model* the way I do. For me that would be a turnoff." So, to each her own! *Similar television preferences: PGHM Meter: 6*

OUTDOORSYNESS

This one poses interesting issues. We have several friends who got quite serious with great guys, only to have the deal break down over his love of the outdoors and her love of, well, creature comforts (such as a roof and a hot shower). Janice once dated a guy who adored boating, hiking, climbing, and riding. In fact, he had a sister who lived in the Alaskan frontier—love of nature ran in his family, big-time! One day, early in the relationship, Dean said to Janice, "C'mon, the dogs want to go for a hike—let's take them out." Janice, who is known to enjoy a walk, but only on pavement, asked Dean, "Do the dogs maybe want to go to the movies, instead?"

Another friend married a guy who likes to go camping. She

told him, "Honey, I'll compromise. I'm happy to go camping, so long as we can come home tonight." What a sport, right? She even removed her "I'm Not Really a Waitress" red nail polish and put on clear. Now, that's a girl who knows how to give in! They've been married for two decades.

On the other side of the spectrum is Shelby, an outdoors-woman extraordinaire. Her Maine-bred, Kennedy-esque family thinks a fun weekend means a tennis tournament, followed by a twenty-mile bike tour, preferably all uphill, and then a competitive evening of playing cards. Her husband, Bill, on the other hand, comes from a more sedentary line of Cubans, who prefer a talk fest on the porch, preferably with some good red wine and cigars. Shelby has taken Bill on more than his share of marathon hikes—and the two have even dubbed a small mountain in New Hampshire "Kill Bill Hill" after a particularly grueling day's climb. The key to their marriage is that Bill really does love the outdoors, and he is happy that his adventuresome wife is able to take him places he never would have ventured to on his own. *Shared appreciation for, or aversion to, the outdoors: PGHM Meter: 7*

ART, BALLET, READING, AND THEATER

It is not necessary to share these interests with your husband. Go to the ballet with your friends. Ditto the museum, the theater, or the book club. Make these your girl-bonding activities and forget trying to involve your guy. Debbie, the former law professor, says that's how to make a marriage last: be sure to get out of the house with your friends from time to time. In other words, constant togetherness is an overrated marital virtue. *Shared interest in culture: PGHM Meter: 3*

IN-LAWS/MOTHER-IN-LAW

We call them the "gift with purchase." They can be a handful, but never fear, we've seen it happen time and time again: they hate you at first and try to make your life miserable. But, when they see you're not going anywhere, they begin to soften. The clincher, however, is when they realize you control access to their grandchildren. Once that realization sinks in, they cave, and, who knows, they may even learn to like you. It happens. Whether you can forgive them for all the bad treatment at the beginning of your relationship—well, that's another story. In other words, bad in-laws suck, but don't let them stop you from marrying the guy. It just won't be easy, but everybody has some kind of cross to bear. This will be yours. *Love of the in-laws: PGHM Meter: 2*

AGE DIFFERENCE

In our humble opinion, based on nothing more than observation, marriages with a big age difference seem to work just fine. If the man is older, chalk it up to male immaturity. They really are big babies, and even a fifteen-year age difference or more barely makes a dent. If the woman is older, it seems to work fine as well. Sure, those women are under a bit more pressure to keep things from sagging but, hell, that may be a good thing. IOHO (in our humble opinion): a nonissue. *Close Age Span: PGHM Meter: 3*

WORK AFTER CHILDREN

Read our lips: no one knows before they have children how they will feel after they have children. Got it? We have seen the biggest workaholics ditch it all a few weeks after giving birth, despite their prior protestations that nothing, and we mean nothing, would keep them from fulfilling their career dreams. We've also seen slacker moms running back to the office at first chance just to be in the presence of other adults and sit in a quiet office with Internet access. So, you can promise whatever you want. You'll do what you need to do whenever you find out what that is. *Agreement on work after kids: PGHM Meter: 3*

POLITICS

We don't know how they do it, but Shriver and Schwarzenegger and Matalin and Carville are not alone. We know several inter-party relationships that work, including one of Janice's friends, a staunch Republican, and her brand-new husband, a bleeding-heart liberal. Frankly, it's beyond us. Maybe they're just strongly sexually compatible. Or able to tune each other out. In either case, you have to know yourself and your own tolerance level. If bleeding-heart liberals make your skin crawl, or if right-wingers are, in your mind, neofascists, don't get in bed with one, OK? *Similar politics: PGHM Meter: 5*

FRIENDS

Everyone we surveyed agrees that he should be OK with your friends. He doesn't have to love them, but he does have to be able to hang with them (or with their spouses/boyfriends, now or future). And if he complains a lot while you're dating, he'll only complain more once you're married. This should be a deal breaker, ladies. *He likes your friends: PGHM Meter: 9*

WHERE TO LIVE

Key—that's your life. If you think you can love somebody and that's it, think again. When Roz, an insurance broker, learned that her boyfriend thought Montana was a great place to relocate, this girl from NYC said: "Mosey along, dude." She married an urbanite and stayed closed to home. Our friend Shelby, on the other hand, loves the peripatetic lifestyle and wisely married an international banker. Their expat lifestyle has kept them moving—from London to Brazil to Singapore—and happy for a few decades. Finally, one of Janice's friends, an inveterate New Yorker, agreed to move to what she called "Greensboring, North Carolina," but she was sure to keep her bachelorette pad in New York as a pied-à-terre for the two of them. *You agree on where to live: PGHM Meter: 7*

CHILDREN OR NO CHILDREN

You should decide in advance whether, for both of you, marriage has to include having (or adopting) children. Especially with second marriages, the children-or-no-children question can be a real deal killer. If he says no and you say yes, going ahead with the marriage anyway can be a very dangerous proposition. And don't think you'll convince him, or worse, trick him into it later. A marriage built on deceit is no marriage at all. One thing that did become clear during our research, however, is this: don't nix a guy from the start just because he has children from a previous marriage. Time and time again, we spoke to women who "never" thought they would marry a man with kids, only to find themselves happily stepparenting. Okay, we don't want to underestimate the difficulties of being a stepparent, but it works just fine in plenty of relationships—better than you would think. So, don't cross him off the list just because he comes with a little baggage of the human variety. *You agree on having kids: PGHM Meter: 10*

MONEY

Jean Chatzky, the *Today Show*'s personal finances expert, says, "It is well-documented that the number-one cause of divorce in the first year of marriage is money. It comes before sex or in-law problems. Money is about power, self-esteem, withholding." In other words, it's really, really important. As the American Academy of Matrimonial Lawyers (that's a pseudonym for "a bunch of divorce lawyers") says, "No matter how rich or how poor a couple is, one of the constant subjects of marital disagreement is money. Whether it's over how money is earned, spent, or saved, money fights are common because money is a part of daily life, from paying the electric bill to saving for retirement." But remember, when you are just starting out, you are just starting out. Miriam, who has been married to her husband for more than fifty years, says, "I never complained to my husband about money in the early days, and we had nothing. When we first got married he would say, 'I want to take you to lunch in Rockefeller Center one day,' and I would just smile. And, you know, it paid off. He makes a fine living today, and even though we've had some hard times we are still very much in love." So make sure you are on the same page in terms of expectations, spending habits, and work ethics. It'll pay off in spades. *You see eye to eye on money: PGHM Meter: 9*

SEX

Our friend Debbie, the "closer" says, "You should always say you just *love* sex before marriage—they can find out the truth later. You love, love, love it. That's how to close the deal!" But the experts, we are sorry to tell Debbie, don't agree. Dr. Laura Berman, the sex doctor, says, "You have to be honest. Many women pretend at first that they want sex as much as the man does, but later, after kids, they may be too tired to do it once a day. If you never had that high a libido, you have to be honest." We agree. Who wants to set a guy up for a rude awakening? That's no way to start a marriage. *You're Aligned When It Comes to the Bedroom: PGHM Meter: 10*

HERE'S HOW TO SCORE ON THE MEET MARKET

Know which options are important to you and buy accordingly.

Know a Guy's History— Is He a Marrier or a Player or, Worst of All, Both?

One last thing when it comes to picking a guy, especially in what we call the secondary market—and by that we mean the second-marriage market: it's essential to know, and understand, a guy's history. The guys trading on the secondary market can come with a lot of baggage, so it's especially important there to know what you're dealing with. But the rules of knowing a guy's history can be useful to any girl who is shopping for a husband, first time or any time. Later, we'll talk more about *how* to research a guy's history. For now, let's discuss *why* it's important to get the lowdown as fast as you can.

Here's what smart shoppers know when it comes to assessing a guy's history: there are, essentially, three types of guys: marriers, just plain players, and marrying players. From the get-go, it is essential to know who you're dealing with—and to get out fast if you're about to buy a lemon. Remember, ladies, there are no lemon laws in the husband trade. Okay, here we go.

Marriers are guys who like to be married. They need a woman who will coordinate their social lives, orchestrate their homes, and just generally provide support. In our estimation, most guys—that's right, most—are marriers. When you meet them, most likely they have just come out of a relationship, and it may have been a pretty long one at that. That's because marriers are almost always in a relationship. Therefore—*ergo*, ladies—marriers are never on the market for long. They enjoy women and the comforts a relationship provides. If you find a marrier and he looks like a good buy, nab him! Act like a fashionista let loose in the Prada outlet of men: elbow the other chicks out of your way and get that guy. Janice and her best single friend, Kim, were once almost mauled in the Prada outlet outside of Florence by a horde of Japanese fashion victims. That's the shopping spirit we are talking about!

Just plain players are what they sound like. These guys don't commit. They like a new flavor of the month, every month. Here's a typical just plain player: his dating history includes girls from every member country of the United Nations. Just plain players get bored easily, and they are never, we repeat never, satisfied. Okay, we'll grant you this: they love you and are very satisfied for about a month. But thereafter, their peripheral vision is in overdrive: they're always scanning the room for a trade-up. Forget these guys, and don't tell yourself that you are going to be the one to convert a player into a marrier. Sure, it appeals to your ego to think you can be the one to do it, but it is beyond an uphill battle. Dating a just plain player is a lost cause. Lemon Law alert: Move on, girl!

Marrying players are the most dangerous characters on the dating landscape. They are only too happy to get married. They love to play house. Kids? Sure, bring 'em on. The more the merrier! Marrying players, unlike just plain players, are willing to tie the knot, and tie the knot they do. But marrying players have a dirty little secret: deep down, they are truly just plain players at heart. They are not satisfied with just one woman, no matter how spectacular that woman is (think Christie Brinkley's husband—if she couldn't keep him, who could?). Marrying players are sometimes hard to detect, so be sure you are open to all the possible signs: a long series of prior marriages or relationships, shady breakup stories, and roving eyes during the courtship process. Marrying players are guys who keep secrets, who have a double life, who keep things on the down low. Your best friends when it comes to uncovering a marrying player are the Internet and the cell phone. We're not exactly saying spy on him, but we are saying keep your eyes open. The HISTORY tab on his computer and the RECENT CALLS on his cell phone—is that spying? Marrying players can be sloppy, so don't let the signs pass you by. We live in a day and age when everything is trackable, so remember: technology is your friend. Use it and you won't become a victim! These guys are lemons to the *n*th degree. If you don't get out fast, you'll be stuck with a big problem.

HERE'S HOW TO SCORE ON THE MEET MARKET

Pick a guy who is a marrier and you won't be standing on the "return line" (check your glossary) anytime soon.

Rule #11:
After-Purchase Repairs and Alterations: Know When the Hems Can Be Altered and the Sleeves Taken Up

No, you won't get everything on your list. Sorry to be the ones who have to break this to you, but as your personal shoppers we feel we must say this: *get over it!*

Even those of you with an unlimited budget (which in the husband-shopping scenario may mean fabulous looks, youth, trophy-wife-worthy credentials, and lots of connections) will not, cannot, find *all* you're looking for. But the beauty of marriage is that you will have a 24-7 opportunity to make minor repairs and alterations, if you can learn to inspire change gently and kindly.

Now, as any good shopper knows, you shouldn't hesitate to buy a dress you love even if it's waaaay too long or the shoulder straps slip or the waist needs to be let out a tad. That's why they invented tailors, right?

But keep this in mind: you wouldn't want to have to turn a

tuxedo into a ball gown, and you can't turn a size 2 into a size 12. We all agree that, as Dr. Dale Atkins puts it, "People fundamentally do not change." But hems and sleeves and other small details? It's our experience that these can be doctored up in no time.

PERSONAL SHOPPER TIP: When the alterations would cost more than the garment, it's time to go back to the store.

You get the analogy? In our lingo, options can be altered. Guts cannot. Basically the rule is that anything fundamental to the guy cannot—or at least should not—be altered. And why would you want to? If you fell in love with a longhaired, guitar-playing free spirit, why would you want to change him into a corporate commando? Dr. Atkins says that if someone wants to present himself to the world in one way, why would you want to alter it? Sure, maybe he'll change himself, over time—we've certainly seen it happen—but do you want to be the catalyst? Nah! That's not tailoring. That's rebuilding.

It is our belief, however, that if you want to teach your hippie hubby to use a little deodorant or to appreciate some creature comforts, that can be done. Just do it gently and take your time. Think of it as a long-term project. Dr. Atkins says that the way to inspire change—and inspire you must because change comes from within—is to do it gently and kindly. First ask yourself: is this really important? More often than not, you'll realize that the way a person looks, the details or options, are not really fundamental. But if you would like to inspire small changes, do so with love. If you can do it that way, we know you'll succeed!

HERE'S HOW TO SCORE ON THE MEET MARKET

Pick the right guy and accept him as he is, but if all of his options don't quite fit your needs, you can try to inspire change. Just make any alterations gently and kindly, and always with love.

Rule #12:
Look for the Right Fit: Must He Be One-of-a-Kind, or Can You Go with Ready-to-Wear?

ONCE YOU have found a guy with good, solid mechanics who seems to be a keeper—a little black dress among men—how do you know he's the one for you? He's kind and makes a good living and doesn't steal and even cleans up after himself. And you're really trying not to be too picky. But isn't there more to it?

When we go shopping, we look for a good fit. A mark of fine cabinetry is tongue-in-groove construction. We look for a dress that fits like a "hand in a glove." Shouldn't the same concept apply to finding a mate?

Plato talked about finding your "other half." Jews talk about finding the *beshert* or destined one. Your mother told you that every pot has a cover. Just about everyone talks about "soul mates." Is there really one person out there who is your true match, the best mate you could find? And what's the chance of finding that one person, that true soul connection? In other words, do we have to go couture or can we find a man off the rack in the ready-to-wear department?

As Susie, a Fort Lauderdale PR pro and cupcake baker extraordinaire, puts it: "There are lots of 'ones' not just '*the* one'. If you are truly open—and your own personal expiration date is coming soon—you will find a guy. It's a question of really being ready."

> **PERSONAL SHOPPER TIP:** The myth of "the one and only" can keep you shopping forever.

"Timing, timing, timing" and "location, location, location." We hear these two mantras again and again from everyone we talk to. If you want to seal the deal, it's not just finding the right guy, but being in the right place at the right time. So, look for men in the likely-to-marry age range (that's why the super-cute twenty-year-old is not a great option if you want to settle down) and shop where someone you'd actually like to marry would actually hang out (think Wall Street watering hole rather than roadside biker bar—unless we have you confused with someone who plans to ride the open road for a few more decades).

In the end, ready-to-wear is the way to go, because searching for that one-of-a-kind guy may keep you shopping, and shopping, and shopping . . . with no end in sight.

HERE'S HOW TO SCORE ON THE MEET MARKET

Is he ready, willing, and able? If so, he may be the buy of your lifetime!

YOUR HANDY PERFORATED SHOPPING LIST
Tear It Out and Carry It with You
So You Don't Make any Mistakes!

— — — — — — — — — — — — — —

Good Guts (these are the musts):

He has a friend or two: ____

He's pretty nice to his mother: ____

No arrest record: ____

Doesn't kick dogs: ____

No imminent need for rehab: ____

Not followed by repo man: ____

Employable: ____

Truthful when it counts: ____

Powerful Engine:

Yes: ____

The Little Black Dress Values (try to get some if not all):

Uglier than me: ____

Known to wash a dish: ____

Let's me have my way (often): ____

Has a degree or two: ____

Not totally wired: ____

Makes a buck: ____

Not a total perv: ____

Not a major downer: ____

Mirror, Mirror (nice if you can get 'em):

Look-alike: ____

From the same hood: ____

Great-grandparents from the same hood: ____

Temperamentally in tune: ____

Personality pairs: ____

Age analogous: ____

Muy simpatico: ____

Good User Interface (pretty much essential):

Listens: ____

Doesn't dominate: ____

Can make me laugh: ____

Doesn't love to argue: ____

Considers my side: ____

Knows when to stop: ____

Your Options (it's all up to you):

Food friend: ____

Educational equal: ____

Sports savvy: ____

TiVo compatible: ____

Outdoorsy (or not): ____

Art aficionado or art avoider (as applicable): ____

In-laws OK: ____

Age appropriate: ____

Working mom supporter: ____

Politically correct: ____

Friendster: ____

Geographically compatible: ____

Kid lover: ____

Money match: ____

Sex *simpatico*: ____

Dating History (super important!):

Marrier—*not* a player ____

— — — — — — — — — — — —

PART II

Where and How to Shop

Now that you know *what* to shop for, you may be wondering where the boys are. Face it: finding a good guy can be harder than finding a ski jacket in a Fourth of July clearance sale, so learning *where* to shop is key.

When we shop for consumer goods nowadays, we face a panoply of shopping venues, each tailored to our every need and then some: malls, outlets, kiosks, online stores, direct-mail catalogues, flea markets, chain stores, department stores, dollar stores, and designer ateliers. But girls-in-the-know learn very quickly how *not* to waste their precious time in the wrong shopping emporium.

Ditto for the husband-shopping pros. Anyone who has been on the singles-bar circuit knows how quickly things can get depressing in that sorry excuse for a dating scene. A bar filled with guys you may—or more likely, may not—have anything in common with is like being in a discount store on a bad day. You've been there, right? The shelves are picked over, what's on them is an unfolded mess, and the scent of body odor hangs pungently in the air. Yuck! It's not fun, and we don't want to send you back there again.

So, listen up. The where-to-shop-for-a-husband question is answered by these three simple words: target, niche, and boutique. Make it your mantra.

It makes sense: the more you can narrow your search to like-minded souls, the more likely you'll quickly find your soul mate. And the good news is, if you stick with your own interests and hobbies—the things that you really like to do—you will find someone who shares those interests and you'll have fun doing it. Ask yourself, where would *I* enjoy being, where can *I* pursue my interests, and where can *I* go to become the best version of myself? As long as it's a place frequented by men (sorry for those of you who enjoy quilting bees or single-sex saunas), we say, go for it!

Still find yourself wishing there was a guidebook to finding men in your area? Well, you have that guidebook; it is already in your hands. Actually, it's in your mouth—we're talking about word-of-mouth. You have to ask, ask, and keep asking everyone you know whether they know a great guy for you. Word of mouth is essential to dating and we'll explain why and how to do it properly.

Finally, you may require a lesson or two in *how* to refine your shopping techniques, especially if you find yourself coming home from the stores empty-handed. Never fear and don't lose faith: your personal shoppers are here to set you on the right track. A few tweaks and adjustments—nothing too painful—and before you know it, you'll be hitting the stores with a vengeance.

Are you ready? Let's find out where and how to shop!

Rule #1:
Shop Online—It Works!

What are you *really* looking for when it comes to a man? Tell us your dirtiest little secrets. Do you like incarcerated men? Vegetarians? Men with STDs? Scientists? Very tall men? Trekkies? Farmers? Indians or born-again Christians? Nice guys who are just a little . . . bipolar?

If so, there is an Internet dating Web site just for you.

Niche dating sites, as they are known, are one of the now-established branches of the already enormous Internet dating industry. Dating on the Web is no longer considered slightly unsavory, and it is certainly no longer a newfangled trend—it is here to stay. Americans are estimated to spend around half-a-billion dollars a year on Internet dating.

In fact, the experts say Internet dating is now in Phase 3.0.

The advent of the big, general dating Web sites—Match .com, eHarmony, and the likes—was Phase 1.0. Match.com calls itself the pioneer; it began in 1995.

Then came Phase 2.0—the niche fillers. And, oh, the niches

they fill! There's Atlasphere.com for Ayn Rand fans, DateMyPet .com for animal lovers, and the aforementioned litany of sites targeted at everyone from Star Trek groupies to vegans. Then, of course, there are the sites focusing on particular religions and ethnic backgrounds, from Armenians to Zoroastrians. The biggest dating Web site community? Shaadi.com, geared for Indian singles, which touts itself as the "world's largest matrimonial service."

The newest trend in Internet dating, Phase 3.0, is the so-called virtual date. You pick an avatar—think video gaming, where you play the game in the form of an animated character that you chose and helped create—and you go on a virtual date with a guy in his own avatar form.

Sound weird? Well, maybe, but the latest thinking is that the act of going on a successful virtual date, say a stroll on the Champs-Elysées or a moonlit walk on the beach (your avatar looks like Angelina Jolie, perhaps, and his looks like Christian Bale as Batman) increases the chances of your actually deciding to meet each other and having a positive real-life date. Who says, you ask? Only a group of MIT and Harvard academics. They claim that virtual dating allows you to "experience" a guy, rather than just evaluate him as if he were a book on Amazon or a pair of shoes on eBay. According to these experts, the interaction that occurs while you move through your virtual date allows you to much more effectively get to know each other than you would if you'd only read each other's profiles in a traditional dating site.

Internet dating is also moving to cell phones, where it is called "mobile dating," and where the interacting takes place by

PERSONAL SHOPPER TIP: Niche dating sites are the boutiques of the dating world. Use them wisely and they may carry just what you are looking for.

text not e-mail, and to instant messaging with video, a prospect that Wired.com speculates may give all the power back to the cheerleaders and jocks.

In any event, you can be sure that just like porn, Internet dating will follow the technology wherever it goes.

Why? Because Internet dating works. Andrew T. Fiore, a University of California at Berkeley academic who is an expert on Internet dating, writes, "The Internet has tremendous potential to help us in our search for partners, whether for a date or for a lifetime. It cuts across social networks to introduce us to people we would never otherwise meet. It offers a catalog of people bigger than any singles group."

Sure, there are some strange dating Web sites out there. ScientificMatch.com purports to compare your immune system with those of the guys in their database and then find you a mate whose immune system is *different* from yours, thus (according to them) yielding healthier babies, all for a fee of just under two thousand dollars. Sorta creepy if you ask us. Motodate.com, another recent entry in the Internet dating market, asks its members to post a sticker on their cars with a four-digit code, thereby enabling other drivers to check them out, and if they like what they see, look them up on the Motodate Web site. This method, according to Motodate, eliminates the "#1 complaint" of Internet daters: photos that look nothing like the person does in real life. Okay, false photos are a real problem, but Motodate doesn't seem like a realistic solution to us.

But most Internet daters stick to the more tried-and-true Internet dating Web sites and rate these sites as pretty helpful. Sixty-four percent of those polled by Pew Research Center agree that online dating can widen your dating pool and help you find a better match. Sixty-one percent of those polled *disagree* with the characterization of online daters as "desperate."

In our opinion, for those last remaining few who still believe

Janice Says . . .

My mother met her second husband through the precursor of Internet dating: *New York* magazine's personal ads. In the ad, Mom focused on her physical assets because, as she puts it, "I know that's what men really want to hear about." It worked, and she got a lot of responses: "In those days, you would go to the post office—you used a P.O. box—and it was like going to the candy store, there would be thirty or more letters waiting." Sid was her fourteenth date. "One man said he didn't want a working woman, so he was out. Others were very nice, but not for me." But Sid, whose letter said, "I'm tall and dark, but you'll have to pass on the hair," was a hit, right from their very first meeting in a Chinese restaurant. Who needs hair, anyway? Sid has lots of other wonderful qualities. They've been happily married now for years.

Internet dating is slightly pathetic and only for losers, it's time to get real. Just ask around and you, too, will hear stories of amazingly successful, interesting, highly credentialed people who have met through Internet dating. How's this sound to you: a Yale-educated attorney who found her scientist husband on Match .com? Yup, she's on her third kid. In fact, thirty million Americans say they know someone who has been in a long-term relationship or is married to someone they met online. If the stories you hear don't convince you that you also aren't "above" putting yourself out there, electronically speaking, we don't know what will.

So just get over it. Dating is a numbers game—and by that we mean the more opportunities you give yourself to meet someone, the more chance you will have of making a match, and a good one at that.

PERSONAL SHOPPER TIP: Get online, *now*! It's all in the numbers. The Internet is a man-shopping mecca, so learn how to master it and you will indeed be a dating diva.

Like everything else, mastering Internet dating takes some doing. Okay, it's not rocket science, but there is a right way and a wrong way to put yourself out there in cyberspace. Fortunately, though, Internet dating has become a playground for social scientists affiliated with some of the finest schools in the country, including MIT and Berkeley. They realize that the Internet has made dating and attraction, perhaps for the first time ever, pretty easily measurable. They can look at who clicks on whose profile and how things work out in the long run. What a treasure trove of data!

So, if the greatest minds of our times are plumbing the depths of the Internet dating field, we thought it would be a good idea to take a look at what they have to say. According to the scientists, here is what works and what doesn't when it comes to dating on the Internet.

1. REMEMBER, HE'S LOOKING FOR HIS MATCH

As we told you earlier (see the mirror-image rule), people are attracted to others who are similar to them. As scientists from MIT put it, "Actual and perceived similarity between potential romantic partners in demographics, attitudes, values, and attractiveness correlate positively with attraction, and later relationship satisfaction." In other words, similarity accounts for both that initial "Wow! She's cute!" and the likelihood of a long and happy marriage. That's why the Internet sites that find guys for you, such as eHarmony and Perfect Match, are largely based on this concept. Their algorithms are rigged to help you find someone just like yourself.

Even if you are not using a site that does the work for you, you can use this rule to your advantage. According to the scientists, you will get a more positive response if you find guys online who are similar to yourself in marital history, desire for children, background, physical build, physical attractiveness, and even smoking habits. These are the criteria of similarity that guys are looking for, according to an MIT study. So, make your profile clear—let it say just who you are—and then when surfing the sites, be sure to pick guys who look like they could be your mirror image. Chances are, they'll be most attracted to you, too.

2. EXTRAVERTED BUT NOT MASCULINE
(CALL IT THE "BE FRIENDLY AND FEMININE RULE")

Even if you find a guy who seems like your perfect mirror image, there are ways of interacting—and presenting yourself in your own profile—that will help to seal the deal. According to social scientists at Berkeley, "For women hoping to attract men online, the data suggest that they will be seen as most attractive when they appear extraverted and not masculine." Extraverted but not masculine? Let's call it friendly and feminine—apparently it works.

Here are our suggestions to you, based on what the latest studies have found:

HOW TO SUCCEED ONLINE:
WHAT MEN FIND ATTRACTIVE

- Send lots of messages to guys.
- Post a picture and make it a good one.
- Self-report that you are attractive.
- Don't volunteer these words: "heavy" or "a few extra pounds."
- Appear extraverted, feminine, and in possession of high self-esteem.

(continued)

- Don't seem self-centered.
- Describe yourself well enough in attitudes, values, and attractiveness to allow a similar guy to find you.

Take your time and make your profile as informative and as attractive as possible. Don't lie, because if you do you're setting yourself up for a quick in-person rejection, but do put your best face and facts forward. And in your Internet interactions, be outgoing and welcoming.

It makes sense. Just take a look at the "most popular" girls on Internet sites. (The sites often rank them, so check it out—it can feel a little like rubbing salt in a wound, but it is educational!) These girls are not always the most beautiful, but they are attractive, have posted a well posed picture, and they sound friendly and, well, nice. After all, a guy wants to know that he has a good chance of being well received and that you aren't a neurotic Pandora's box just waiting to be unlatched. Have a good friend or relative check out your photo—or have a professional one taken (you'll find plenty of Internet-profile photographers online)—and carefully write a description of yourself that is accurate but takes into account a guy's perspective (and not in a weird, overtly sexy, or desperate way, OK?). Ask an honest friend to read it and tell you whether your profile sounds like you, isn't too negative, and doesn't have any other husband-shopping defects.

We have to take a moment here and acknowledge that Inter-

AND WHAT ARE WE WOMEN LOOKING FOR IN OUR ONLINE MEN?

You may be embarrassed on behalf of womankind to hear this, but researchers from the University of Chicago and MIT, who studied more than twenty thousand online daters, have found that what women are looking for in a man is (drum roll, please) money . . . but they'll take height if they can't get the big bucks. Yes, according to the study, a six-foot tall man will be more successful than a shorter man. But, if, let's say, a five-foot tall guy reports that he makes $325,000 *more* than the six-foot-tall man, height, schmeight: the two will be equally successful on the Internet dating market.

net dating is not as easy as nabbing a vintage dress on eBay using PayPal. There are plenty of problems on the Internet dating front, some quite serious. There are schemers who defraud women by posing as smitten but poor paramours. There are married men hoping for a quick score. There are sites that have been accused of baiting women by posting false profiles. There are sites with a serious imbalance in the male-to-female ratio, and there are sites that don't let you see what's on them until after you have subscribed. As in all else, you must keep your common sense switched on when using online dating sites. These are the types of rip-offs and scams we see in just about every industry. So, a smart Internet dater is one who is informed and is ready to deal with the downside of dating online.

AVOIDING THE PITFALLS:
THE TROUBLE WITH INTERNET DATING

According to the Better Business Bureau, safety is a concern in online dating. Take the following steps to protect yourself, and always use your common sense:

- Do not reveal any personal information in your online dating profile, in your personal ads, or in your private e-mails to other singles. Such information includes your real name, specifics about where you live, or any other info that could be used maliciously.

- Use only the communication tools provided by the dating service. You should not invite singles to e-mail you at your regular e-mail address, at least until you know them better.

- When you e-mail singles in private, consider using an anonymous e-mail account at a free site.

PERSONAL SHOPPER TIP: The #1 most important Internet dating advice is this—only agree to meet a guy in a public place, preferably with a friend nearby, and for a short time only. And, as always, listen to your gut and do your research! This is where it really pays off.

THE PROBLEM MEN
OF INTERNET DATING:
WATCH OUT FOR THEM!

The serial searchers

The chemistry deprived

and

The liars and the insincere

Safety is not the only concern online. You also have to be sure you don't waste your valuable time. We surveyed a group of twenty-five- to thirty-year-old women, a group that has come of age with Internet dating. Although Internet dating has no stigma in their crowd (they all claimed to have several friends who met boyfriends—if not husbands—online), they pointed out three significant categories of problem guys who pop up on dating Web sites all the time.

Let's discuss:

SERIAL SEARCHERS

These problem men are simply picky daters—you know, most everyone you know—in their online manifestation. Serial searchers are always thinking to themselves, "Hmm. Maybe I can find someone better. . . ." They love online dating because serial searchers are, by definition, addicted to clicking. You haven't heard of "click addiction?" We can explain it this way: you know that feeling you get when you've been online too long, scrolling, scrolling, scrolling? Your eyes feel kinda papery and your head feels sorta dizzy? Well, these symptoms evidently don't affect those with click addiction. They never tire. Never! That compulsive drive to find the best mate, and their ability to search and search and search—it's unceasing. They are long-distance scrollers, marathon surfers, and the iron men of the Internet. When a serial searcher hits the dating Web sites, well, picture a kid with ADD in a Chucky Cheese. Sure, they may e-mail you—you and dozens of other thirty-to-thirty-five-year-olds. An e-mail from one of these guys is worthless—it is valueless dating currency. The exchange rate is as follows: two gazillion e-mails from a serial searcher is equivalent to one e-mail from a nice guy. The problem is, it's hard to spot a serial searcher immediately.

Serial searchers seem great—they've got the lingo down. Their e-mails are funny and enticing. After all, they've had a lot of practice. But after a few days of correspondence, when it's time to, shall we say, "get off the pot," well, they don't. So be wary of serial searchers and don't let them drag you down. They are an inevitable by-product of Internet dating, one to be dismissed without a second thought.

THE CHEMISTRY DEPRIVED

No, don't worry, we're not talking atomic numbers or valence electrons. We're talking sexual chemistry. The problem is, it can't be assessed online. Not really. If we put aside those liars who post deceptive photographs, looks can be judged to some degree of accuracy. But looks do not equal chemistry. The world is much more complicated than that, so judging chemistry is the final frontier of Internet dating.

Sure, the scientific community is all over this one, but, despite all best efforts, no one has come up with a way to translate that little feeling of excitement you get on the back of your neck when you see a guy who does it for you into a parameter that can be expressed in an online profile and transmitted over the Internet. Hopes have been placed on virtual dating and digital photography and nuanced profile writing. Bloggers speculate about the advent, one day in the future, of smell-o-vision and pheromone-transmitting computers. Sounds like a dream to us. In the meantime, you'll just have to narrow down the guys you want to correspond with based on shared interests and good looks—and the chemistry question will have to be addressed through trial-and-error, in-person meetings, the good, old-fashioned way.

LIARS

Is it any surprise that in a world where private-college admissions counselors are paid upward of thirty thousand dollars to help an eighteen-year-old write a college essay about their "life experiences" that an industry of dating-profile writers and advisors has sprung up? No, of course not. Our favorite is the aptly named e-cyrano.com. (The real-life Cyrano died in 1655!) Just as college admissions are getting more and more competitive each year, so, apparently, is Internet dating. Why else would plagiarism be a growing problem in the Internet dating world? As *The Wall Street Journal* not long ago reported, there is a burgeoning business in a new type of identity theft: someone who steals your cool online personality. Certain distinctive phrases have been spreading like wildfire throughout the world of Internet dating Web sites—a phenomenon that can't be explained purely by coincidence. The plagiarists are just one of many types of liars online.

Then there are the guys whose pictures look nothing like

they do in real life. One friend swears off these guys from the get-go; she asks herself, if they are willing to be so deceitful with their photos, what else will they lie about? We think this is a good policy. After all, we can forgive a little aging and perhaps some wear and tear, but when a guy's picture is a decade old—or worse, is a picture of his good-looking cousin—we say, end the meeting quickly and move on with your life. In fact, *Scientific American* reports that 20 percent of online daters admit to deception, "and if you ask them how many other people are lying, however—an interviewing tactic that probably gets closer to the truth—that number jumps to 90 percent."

And what do people lie about online? Pretty much everything: marital status, age, weight, income, religion. You name it.

With all of these problems, yes, Internet dating can be tough; you need to develop something of a thick skin. Even the most exciting and romantic exchange of e-mails can sometimes presage a major letdown upon meeting. And you never know what you'll hear when you move from e-mail to phone. Kay Unger, the fashion designer, got to this point in a phone call with a guy: "We were talking and it seemed OK until he asked me where I live. I said 'downtown,' and he told me we were 'geographically incompatible' and hung up." Jeez! We also recently heard a story about a senior-citizen date that made our hair stand on end: the man's underwhelmed expression upon meeting the woman caused her to ask, "Should I leave now?" Yikes!

So, no, Internet dating isn't always easy. But it can be worth the trouble if you learn to use it wisely. Here's our advice: get tough, don't expect too much—and maybe you'll be pleasantly surprised. Because for every yucky Internet dating story, there is a great Internet dating story, and with careful screening (see Part

How to Shop for a Husband

III Rule #1: Do Your Research), plenty of contact pre-date, and a public (and short) first meeting, you should do just fine.

And if the guy you meet doesn't spin your wheels, maybe you can fix him up with a friend, and he can do the same for you!

HERE'S HOW TO SCORE ON THE MEET MARKET

Come to terms with Internet dating, because online shopping for men is here to stay.

HOW *NOT* TO FIND A MAN

Our dear friend Tara, a reporter and producer in Miami, who is so fabulous, so plugged in, and so trendy that she is known professionally as "the trend tracker," met a guy in what has to be *the* least probable way. She misdialed. That's right. She was one digit off.

Okay, here's how it went. Tara came home one night, exhausted from a long day of work, collapsed on her couch, and began channel surfing. For some inexplicable reason, she settled on the Miss Hawaiian Tropic Contest. Don't ask—we said she was really tired! Anyway, Tara zoned out until the interview portion of the show, when her interest was piqued. Could it be? Did one of the contestants just say that the *most* important invention of the last hundred years was self-tanner? Tara couldn't take it! She *had* to call her equally fabulous decorator friend, Jeff, and share the idiocy.

(continued)

So she dialed and barely waited for Jeff to answer: "You are never going to believe this! I'm watching this show and . . ." Well, Tara didn't realize she had misdialed until Mr. Misdial spoke up. The ensuing telephone conversation, in which Tara's witty repartee was returned, stroke by stroke, by Mr. Misdial's parries, was so great, it turned into a week of texting, e-mailing, and finally, phone conversations. He seemed perfect: smart, funny to the point of hilarity, and super-interested in Tara. After putting him off for over a week, Tara agreed to finally meet Mr. Misdial—in a well-lit neighborhood restaurant where she is known. Smart girl.

Suffice it to say, it was a great date. Even Mr. Misdial had to stop the torrent of conversation to say, in the middle of dinner, "This is going *really* well, isn't it?" Tara played her cards right and after a not-so-chaste kiss in the car, refused further activity and went home, a very happy camper. E-mails followed, as did phone calls and texts and the promise of many future dates.

A week later, the e-mails went from a waterfall to a trickle. Then the calls petered out. Finally, the texts stopped. No explanations. Mr. Misdial went on a business trip and promised, by e-mail, to call when he returned. Tara never heard from him again.

What the . . . ?

The only conclusion that we can draw is that Tara had waaaaay too little info on this dude. She needed to do her research. Someone in Miami must have known him—

after all, she knows everyone. Surely, this isn't the first time this guy came on like a storm and petered out like a sun shower. No way. If Tara had had the chance to talk to somebody—anybody—who knew this guy, she probably would have gotten a story. A not-so-pretty story. But when you misdial, you have no context: no common friends, no work acquaintances, no base of interests. All you have that draws you together is that one missed digit.

And, obviously, that isn't enough.

Tara's misdialing misadventure has a parallel in the consumer fraud world. It's called the "fat finger scam": these creeps count on people who misdial a phone number or mistakenly enter a misspelled Internet address. Example: 1-800-COLECCT for 1-800-COLLECT. They trade off of our mistakes and siphon customers off of reputable businesses. It's a scam! Don't fall for it!

Rule #2:
Be a Bricks-and-Mortar Dater

We can tell you one thing for certain. If you live in Ireland, go to your local pub, and if you're visiting Ireland, it's time for a pint. We offer this advice because a recent study of marriage in Ireland revealed that 23 percent of Irish newlyweds met in a pub. That's almost a quarter of the newly married population in Ireland! Now that's good odds.

In the United States, though, bricks-and-mortar dating is a little more complicated. There is no one place in which a majority—or even a strong plurality—of singles seem to be meeting their significant others. So what's a girl to do?

Well, what a girl is *not* to do is to depend on those pathetic vacations, dances, and bar nights pitched at singles. Do they ever work? No.

Singles vacations? Filled with women. Women, women, and more women! And when you *do* find a guy on one of these trips, he is there, as Erica, an attorney, puts it, "just to get laid." Not to put too fine a point on it, but she's right.

Singles bars or singles nights at bars? Yuck. Been there, done that, they stink.

Singles dances? Double yuck. Too much competition, too many people, too frantic, too too. Forget them.

So are we left to meet online and online only?

Of course not.

There are certain places that are still good venues for meeting men. Here are our favorites:

Elite-Status Airport Lounges. Although it does seem that nowadays, everyone and their brother can get into these elite airport lounges, we still think they are great places to meet guys. Caveat number one: they may be married. Caveat number two: they may be just looking for a little somethin' strange and will return to their girlfriend of five years as soon as the plane departs. On the other hand, the guys in these lounges are usually well-employed, well-educated, well-paid, and they have time on their hands (at least while in the lounge). So don't write them off. Remember: you can buy a day pass, so if you have a long layover, it might be worth trying. And if you don't meet a guy, these are pretty good places to spot a celebrity or two.

Airplanes. Forget the lounge, what about the plane itself? Although we have only anecdotal evidence upon which to rely, airplanes seem to us to be a great place to meet guys. In fact, we know of several marriages that have resulted from seatmate situations. Melissa, a *Today Show* producer, met her husband after he asked the flight attendant to move his seat near Melissa's (even though they hadn't, as yet, met). He struck up a conversation,

PERSONAL SHOPPER TIP: Want to avoid an awkward call? Try SlyDial.com, a service that will allow you to leave him a message by going directly to voicemail, without having to actually speak person-to-person. We'd never recommend it for a long-term relationship, but if a fix-up goes wrong, or an Internet communication is going nowhere fast, you have our permission to ditch him via SlyDial.

but Melissa wasn't interested. He even followed her to an Oktoberfest celebration in Munich—their destination—but she still didn't deem him date-worthy. Melissa's future husband, now a prominent orthopedic surgeon, wasn't taking no for an answer. He managed to keep the relationship going, somehow, after returning to the States. Slowly, she began to come around. Even though she lived in Indiana and he lived in New York, he FedExed her round-trip tickets so she could visit. This was truly an airplane relationship. After seven months of weekend visits, she moved to New York and they married a year later. So, don't wear your ugly gray sweats and your hair in a scrunchy on that all-night flight to Rio, OK? You never know who is going to be on the plane.

Work. Gone are the days when you couldn't date your boss, your colleague, or your client. And we say, good riddance! After all, no one stays in the same job for life anymore, and there are too many good opportunities to meet someone at work, so don't rule out work as a place to meet guys. If you work long, long hours, as so many of us do, work is an especially great place—maybe *the* place—to meet men. So put on some lipstick, don't walk around looking shlubby, and have a positive attitude, and if the guys you work with are married, losers, or total geeks, then remember the magic words: "Do you have a friend for me?" Even geeky married losers can have a nice friend or cousin. Really, they can.

MEETING CUTE

The "meet cute" is a Hollywood convention in which the main characters meet in an unlikely, amusing, or offbeat way. Usually found in screwball comedies, those who meet cute almost always end up living HEA (happily ever after, duh!). In *Singin' in the Rain* Gene Kelly literally falls into Debbie Reynolds's convertible while running to escape aggressive fans. In *Notting Hill* Hugh Grant meets Julia Roberts by spilling orange juice on her. And in *It Happened One Night,* Clark Gable and Claudette Colbert meet fighting over the last seat in a bus.

Weddings. You are dressed up and looking fine. You know the people, or at least some of them. You have a glass of wine and there's a band playing the corniest songs ever ("YMCA" anyone?). Morever, and perhaps most importantly, you know exactly who is single and who is not. Plus, there's no pressure—you are there for a joyful purpose. How good does that sound? It sounds good and it's called a wedding. We're almost inclined to tell you to wedding-crash, but we won't go quite that far. Of course, you could always think of it yourself. Right?

Alumni Events. Although we know of no scientific study measuring the number-one place to meet guys who you may actually end up marrying, we would venture to guess that alumni events—particularly for the slightly older, secondary market (check your glossary!)—are up there. There must be something about that shared history, common background, or maybe it's just plain nostalgia. Whatever. If you miss an alumni event you do so at your own peril. We're telling you, this is the place! And if your alma mater isn't organized, then you are just the one to get things going. Think of all the phone calls you can make and the expansion of your circle to all these old friends who can fix you up. It's a beautiful thing.

Classes. It worked for Janice. There's nothing like *not* trying. Just pick a subject in which you are truly interested, put away all worries about men, and throw yourself into something you'd really like to learn. When you least expect it, you never know what can happen.

HERE'S HOW TO SCORE ON THE MEET MARKET

No singles events for you: just frequent those places where you will meet guys who share your interests and who are of the caliber to which you'd like to become accustomed. That's how to nab the guy of your dreams.

Rule #3:
Speed Dating Is
the Way to Go

Is it just us, or does it seem to you, too, that thousands of years from now, when historians look back to America in the early 2000s, the act of speed dating will be considered one of the more bizarre rituals of contemporary life? Come on: adults playing musical chairs, with a timer set, in an attempt to meet their lifelong mates?

Speed dating *is* a little strange, but it may surprise you that it has become something of a favorite of social scientists who study relationships and dating. They say that speed dating actually works, and it works even better than online dating.

Look, dating is a numbers game, we can all agree on that, right? Like smart marketers or advertisers, we need to look at both the size of the audience, the number of men we meet, and the yield, or the number of dates that result. In other words, we need to get "seen" by a lot of men, but we also need to place ourselves in a medium where the chances of a follow-up date are good.

Janice Says . . .

Speaking of musical chairs, my then-single friend and producer, Kim, and I used to say that our *lives* felt like a game of musical chairs, where all of our friends had grabbed a chair—meaning a husband—and we were stuck standing when the music stopped! Well, don't let the music stop while you're still standing. Get out there, go on blind dates, speed date, whatever . . . and you won't be the last girl standing!

So compare these stats: *The New York Times* reports that "customers of online dating services typically end up going out with fewer than 1 percent of the people whose profiles they study online. But something very different happens at a speed-dating event. The average participant makes a match with at least 1 in 10 of the people they meet; some studies have found the average is 2 or 3 out of 10."

1, 2, or 3 out of 10? If those were statistics for coming down with a disease, you'd be terrified, right? But we want this disease! It's a dating epidemic, so bring it on. Speed dating works.

That's the good news. The not-so-good news is that speed dating does follow the same trend as online dating. Men are looking for good looks in their women, while women are seeking wealth and status in their men. This somewhat depressing and seemingly old-world phenomenon is often chalked up to evolution: women historically have stayed home and nurtured the babies, and therefore look for a spouse who is a good provider (hence the search for wealth and status). Men's interest is in propagating the species in their own image (and therefore through their own seed) and seek healthy young women who are likely to be nice and fertile—and whose health and youth may be best evidenced by their good looks. As Martie G. Haselton, Ph.D., a UCLA psychologist, told *Time* magazine, romantic love is a "commitment device," an evolutionary necessity developed by "natural selection [that] has built love to make us feel romantic" and more likely to develop bonds that will produce children. Romantic love also makes us stay together long enough to raise those children to their own reproductive age.

So, looks are important, but the beauty of speed dating is that men who speed date seem to go one more step: they don't quite as quickly write off those who don't best meet the looks criteria. Instead, they seem to give a girl a second glance. This is how the experts account for the higher yield in speed dating than in Internet dating.

Speculation is rife: why do speed daters forgive the less well-endowed in the looks department while online daters do not? It is thought that if people meet face to face, they are more likely to be seduced by chemistry or maybe even good old-fashioned personality. Evidently, men will look past the looks if they have to get to know you, even for a few minutes. Nice, huh? In fact, in the speed-dating world, women are pickier than men! We love that.

In addition, studies show that the decision to date someone is always made quickly—in a few minutes or less—so speed dating is an economical way of doing what we all do anyway, which is make quick judgments about guys we'd like to see again.

But here's something to keep in mind, and it comes from the hallowed halls of Northwestern University and the Massachusetts Institute of Technology. Researchers there say that it is important for a girl not to appear unselective (we like to call it desperate) in a speed-dating scenario. Here's how the scientists put it: "The negative generalized-reciprocity correlation was partially mediated by perceived unselectivity." Huh? Why don't they just say it like it is: if you appear to be desperate, no one (or very few guys) will want you. Got it?

PERSONAL SHOPPER TIP: Don't appear unselective—aka desperate! No one wants to be "chosen" by someone who has no standards. In speed dating, seeming a little picky is a positive.

This is where that pickiness we talked about earlier can be used to your advantage. Don't use pickiness offensively, use it defensively: don't eliminate a world of guys because they don't know that Houston Street in New York City is pronounced "How-ston," but do appear to be selective when in the presence of men. In other words: don't eliminate guys arbitrarily, but eliminate them to your advantage. Show them that you are a choosy girl who is worthy of the best.

HERE'S HOW TO SCORE ON THE MEET MARKET

Speed dating may seem weird, but it is a marketplace where a girl can get a second look and where guys show that maybe it's not just looks that count.

Rule #4:
Word of Mouth:
Persistence Pays

We would like to talk to you now about what we believe is a civic obligation that every citizen has; nay, it is more—we are talking about an inalienable and nontransferrable responsibility that we all inherit, simply by virtue of being human! We hold this truth to be self-evident, and we hope you do, too:

You must help your single friends out by fixing them up. And they must do the same for you.

Fix-ups, blind dates—do you associate them with desperation? Do you think to yourself that only really hard-up people need to beg for dates? Do you in your heart of hearts think that blind dates are embarrassing, creepy, and a little bit weird?

Well, if these are your thoughts that we are channeling, we have three words for you:

Get over yourself!

We understand that asking for and going on a blind date means making yourself vulnerable. It means you have to tell someone—and we're recommending you tell pretty much everyone you know—"I'd like to be fixed up." This is vulnerability point number one. Then, you have to show up at a date, sight unseen—this is vulnerability point number two. We're not saying this is easy. In fact, we understand very well that it is *not* easy. But we are saying it is necessary.

Why? Because fix-ups are one of the most successful means of meeting guys. And that is simply because blind dates and setups are like having dozens of personal shoppers at your disposal. What's more, these personal shoppers often (but not always) know you well and know your taste. So, what could be better than that? Besides, it is said that the fastest way to get to heaven is to make a successful match, so who are we to snub our noses at a route to eternal bliss?

Some people are just good at making matches. They are like personal shoppers who keep their clients' needs in mind when all the new stuff comes in to the store. It's like those women who make friends with salesgirls at lots of stores—that way they keep you in mind when things you like go on sale. Similarly, every single girl should make friends with people who are good novice matchmakers and who know lots of people. That way, when a good buy comes on the market, the fixer-uppers will be thinking of you. Every single girl needs in her close circle a couple of friends who enjoy fixing people up and have had some success doing it.

Shari Gersten is one of those people. A lawyer and headhunter by profession, she has made eight—count them, eight—successful matches. She says, "I set up my brother in five minutes.

THEY WERE FIRST: ISAAC AND REBEKAH

According to the Bible, the very first couple to be "fixed up" by someone else was Isaac and Rebekah. In Genesis, the story goes that Abraham sent his trusted servant, Eliezar, to his hometown to find a match for his son, Isaac. Luckily for all involved, Abraham told the servant that the Lord would send an angel to guide him. And, apparently, so he did. Eliezar, though, didn't want to make any mistakes. He prayed to God and asked for a sign: specifically, the right girl should not only offer Eliezar water but should offer his camels water, too. Now, that would be a nice girl! Well, lo and behold, Rebekah fit the bill. A generous, water-proffering virgin, she was from the right town and "very fair to look upon," too. Significantly, Rebekah's family did not just send her off to marry Isaac without consulting her (even though Eliezar showered them with some pretty snazzy gifts—we're talking shekels and raiment galore), she is asked whether she wishes to go. Rebekah agreed and, as they say, the rest is history.

Biblical lessons for single women? Well, how about these: be nice to the help, generosity is key, be kind to animals . . . and don't be averse to being fixed up!

I said to the woman, 'You are going to marry my brother.' There was a commonality, good timing, and interest. It's all about expanding your circles. Just the way you network in business, you have to let people know you are looking. Take a chance, be

PERSONAL SHOPPER TIP: Fix up others as you would have them fix you up.

vulnerable. And remember, you are not at the top of other people's minds all the time, so remind them and ask: 'Do you know someone for me?' "

Gersten also suggests that you ask for feedback. In other words, if you get set up, steel yourself and ask the matchmaker, "What did he think of me?" Even if you didn't like him, you may learn something. For example, Gersten says that you might learn that you talk too much about work, or appear too serious, or unknowingly go on and on about your ex-boyfriends. It may be painful to hear, but once you know how you come across on a date, you can take steps to fix those little quirks. The matchmakers know!

Janice Says . . .

In my opinion, fixing people up is an obligation of all happily married or attached people. When I found Steve, I just couldn't bear the idea that Kim, my dear friend with whom I spent almost every second of my single years, would be alone. "We have to get Kim married," I told Lizzie, my sister. So Lizzie, who worked at a large bank, remembered that one of the bankers there,

Tom, had recently separated from his wife. "Okay, you can fix them up," Lizzie said. "But she'd better be nice—I have to work with him!" I promised, crossed my fingers, and made Kim swear she wouldn't lose Lizzie her job. As it turns out, Kim *was* nice . . . so nice, in fact, that she is happily married to the guy today and a stepmom to his three kids. And Tom, well, he happened to be an awfully good catch: tall, dark, handsome, and very successful.

But Kim and Tom are not the only successful fix-up in my matchmaking career. I also set up Kay Unger, the designer, with one of Steve's friends. They've been a happy couple for years now and are going strong.

In fact, I'm always thinking about my single friends and acquaintances.

Not long ago, my son David developed a fascination with bones—probably after learning about dinosaurs. When a friend, who is an orthopedic surgeon, offered to show David some X-rays, we jumped at the chance. At the doctor's office, we passed the office of one of his colleagues. "He's recently single," my friend said. "You wouldn't know anyone to fix him up with, would you?" Well, yes I did! After checking out the newly single doctor's picture, I thought of Kay Unger's adorable assistant. And yes, today they are married.

Three matches so far, and more to come, I hope. So, get inspired! You, too, can be a successful matchmaker. When it works, it feels really good.

HERE'S HOW TO SCORE ON THE MEET MARKET

Some people are just good at making matches—they are the personal shoppers of the dating world. Befriend them and watch your dating life take off!

Rule #5:
Find Out Where
the Boys Are

Okay. You work in publishing. Or retail. Or PR. Or teaching. Or design. Or television. Or in a museum, a library, a foundation. Or advertising.

What's our point? You, like so many women out there, work in a ghetto . . . a "girl ghetto." Have you noticed?

Unfortunately, many women gravitate to the same professions. If you're the type who likes the company of women, working in these environments can be a blast: it's almost like working in a sorority house. But if you're looking to meet a guy, your workplace is not exactly fertile ground. That means for eight, nine, ten, or more hours of the day, you are not going to be exposed to potential dating material (although remember Rule #4 and always make your friends and colleagues aware that you would greatly appreciate being fixed up with anyone they may deem fit!).

What's a girl to do?

You need to spend some time in the men's department.

The men's department, in our lingo, is where the boys are. So let's play our numbers right, ladies, and see where the men are hanging out. We're looking for critical mass!

Here's our top-ten list of where to find guys in numbers that make the odds look pretty good:

1. The Apple Store. Maybe they tend toward the geeky and maybe they skew a little young, but no woman can walk into an Apple Store and not remark on the sheer number of men there. Geez, guys, where have you been? Hallelujah! Even *Cosmopolitan* magazine suggests it as a place to find men in critical mass. The Apple Store gives classes of all kinds, so maybe you can finally organize those digital photos while you're perusing the male merchandise. And remember, we've already told you that you shouldn't turn your nose up at the nerdy (see Part I, Rule #1). They make good husbands and are really just smart guys who need a little fashion advice. And it's not just Apple: think Home Depot, Sports Authority, Best Buy. You get the idea, right?

2. Fly Fishing. How many friends of yours have been on vacations—especially those that purport to be "singles trips"—only to report on a male-female ratio that would be almost equal to, like, zero? Forget it. Men don't seem to visit cities or even cultural spots when left to their own devices. Instead they go on "guy trips" such as fly fishing, golf clinics, white-water rafting, or skiing. Now, we're not telling you to take up extreme frisbee if that's not of interest to you, but if you'd just as soon enjoy the great outdoors as visit the museums of Italy, then go where the guys are. Just try it. You might develop a life-long passion for trout that you never knew you had. Ute, a yoga instructor from Astoria, Oregon, goes fly fishing in Wyoming with a group of women friends once a year and has grown to love the sport. "I can't tell you how many men have come up to me when they see me with my fly fishing gear in the airport. It's an ice breaker." Doesn't hurt that she's five-foot-eight, blond, and in amazing shape. Whatever.

3. Think "T" for a Degree: Taxes, Technology, and Trading. Just as we women have our industries of choice, so do men. They trend toward jobs in the technology and finance industries. So, if you have any reason to get an advanced degree, how about an LLM in tax law, an MBA in finance, or a MS in computer science? Okay, a degree in nuclear engineering may not be in the cards for you, but if there's an MBA program near where you live, find out where the students hang out, start to have lunch in a nearby restaurant, or go to their bookstore. Why not? It wouldn't kill you....

PERSONAL SHOPPER TIP: A friend who has a boyfriend has access into a world of men—his friends. She is under a moral obligation to share the wealth!

4. Thinking of Relocating? Think Techy Cities. No, not everyone is going to pack up and start over in another city (certainly not just to get a date on Saturday night), but if you *are* in the market to relocate, why not choose a city where the ratio of men to women is not, well, appalling? *Men's Health* did a study recently of the best cities in which to find a mate, and not surprisingly, the high-tech cities of San Jose and San Francisco, California, and Raleigh, North Carolina, fared well. The percentage of men in high-tech jobs is ridiculous; some studies say only 11 percent of high-tech workers are women! Just something to think about.

5. Get Out of the Ghetto. Are you in a position where you could take your skills to a more male-dominated industry? For example, are you in public relations or human resources? Well, you don't have to do PR for a women's magazine or HR for a performing arts center. Think investment bank. Think major law firm. Think hospital. You'll probably make more money there, anyway.

In sum, we don't know if it's nature or nurture (although we'd venture to guess it's probably both), but we do know that women tend to drift toward traditionally female industries. So, if you want to shake things up a little—and meet a guy—you owe it to yourself to explore the men's department. You might even find that things on that floor fit you better, or can be cinched with a belt, or worn with a skirt to make a real fashion statement! We say, go for it.

HERE'S HOW TO SCORE ON THE MEET MARKET

Get out of the girl ghetto and shop in the men's department if you want to come home with a man!

Rule #6:
Professional Matchmakers and Matchmaking Services May (or May Not) Be Worth Your While

Leave it to Singapore. Clean, safe, a little-bit-Big-Brothery Singapore. It is the only country (at least as far as we know) with a government-run matchmaking service. Known as the "Social Development Unit," this service is intended to encourage marriage in the small city-nation. So Singapore may be the only sovereign country that moonlights as a yenta. Yes, ladies, the government of Singapore has a Ministry of Health, an Economic Development Board . . . and a Web site called "Love-Byte.org." Singaporeans are invited to singles weekends, encouraged to avail themselves of free makeover sessions, asked for their "hot success stores," and are able to e-mail "Dr. Love," who is probably the only "doctor of love" who is also a civil servant.

While other countries and ethnic groups aren't as forthright about their matchmaking as Singapore is, many others do encourage a reconnection with the homeland that often results in a love match. For example, Irish Way, Birthright Armenia, Taglit-Birthright Israel, and the Expatriate Youth Summer Formosa Study Tour of Taiwan all bring young people together with others of a similar background, and sometimes love is in the air.

Hmm. If small countries can become matchmakers, does this mean matchmakers can run small countries? We wouldn't be surprised.

Professional matchmakers are paid to accomplish the nearly impossible: they sniff out that thing called chemistry and make it work to your advantage. If you really want to ramp up your dating chances, you may want to consult a professional.

And what exactly, you may ask, makes them professionals?

We're glad you asked.

Let us put it this way: if you had the opportunity to ask the yenta from *Fiddler on the Roof* what her qualifications were, you wouldn't expect her to tell you she had a degree in matchmaking, would you? Well, professional matchmakers today are, for better or worse, no yentas. They have more in common with headhunters than they do with the babushka-clad old ladies of our collective unconscious. If you hire a professional matchmaker in the twenty-first century, you may want to know whether or not they are certified by the Matchmaking Institute, an organization that purports to provide "intensive training" to matchmakers in all aspects of their trade and to issue certifications in matchmaking. Can this stuff be taught? The founders of this New York City school think it can.

BE THANKFUL YOU LIVE IN THE TWENTY-FIRST CENTURY!

DATING IN VICTORIAN ENGLAND WAS NO PIECE OF CAKE . . .

At nineteen and twenty and twenty-one she had thought that all the world was before her. With her commanding figure, regular long features, and bright complexion, she had regarded herself as one of the beauties of the day, and had considered herself entitled to demand wealth and a coronet. At twenty-two, twenty-three, and twenty-four any young peer, or peer's eldest son, with a house in town and in the country, might have sufficed. Twenty-five and -six had been the years for baronets and squires; and even a leading fashionable lawyer or two had been marked by her as sufficient since that time. But now she was aware that hitherto she had always fixed her price a little too high. On three things she was still determined—that she would not be poor, that she would not be banished from London, and that she would not be an old maid.

—Anthony Trollope, *The Way We Live Now*, 1875

According to the experts, there are about 1,600 professional matchmakers in the United States and the profession is growing. Any thoughts that the Internet would clear the field have been put to rest: the rampant dishonesty and the overwhelming size of the dating pool online have kept the yenta business flourishing.

Professional matchmakers promise a personalized approach that works; the Matchmaking Institute says, "you should expect to make some kind of meaningful connection within the first three or four introductions" made by a certified matchmaker. Not bad, huh?

The Better Business Bureau, however, has other things to say: "There may be some specific problems associated with the industry," a representative told *USA Today*. Complaints against matchmakers (and other dating services) are increasing dramatically each year.

Hiring a matchmaker is almost like hiring a hairdresser or a housekeeper: there are almost no generalizations that can be made about them as a group. One can be great and the next just awful, or worse, a scammer.

So here's the thing: some matchmakers are relatively cheap, charging a flat monthly fee, and some are outrageously expensive, and charge by the fix-up. Some are talented at what they do and claim excellent track records, others are fly-by-night con artists. Some accept male and female clients and many just accept male clients. You see what we mean? This is a field in which a good referral from a trusted friend and a positive gut feeling can mean a lot. You kinda have to have chemistry with your matchmaker.

PERSONAL SHOPPER TIP: Meeting a matchmaker who has a male-only clientele may be a free way to get access to a lot of great dates!

What matchmakers can offer is the personal touch. They should have met all of the men they fix you up with. They should also have vetted those guys, checked for any criminal records and, certainly, verified the guy's marital status. They also should (and notice we said "should") be the kind of people who can assess chemistry and have an intuitive feel for that certain *je ne sais quoi*. Professional matchmakers are the casting directors in the movie of life, if you see what we mean. That's not an easy job description to fill.

Matchmakers can also function as dating doctors. A good matchmaker will get feedback from all of your dates and let you know if you blab about yourself too much, or if you have nasty table manners, or if you just don't convey your interest in a guy effectively enough. Used properly, this information may be enough to remedy your dating woes.

So, if you want to hire a matchmaker and do things the shtetl way, be our guest. Just do your homework and make sure you are not throwing your money out the window.

HERE'S HOW TO SCORE ON THE MEET MARKET

Want to catch yourself a catch? Find yourself a find? You may need a professional, one who knows how to make a match.

ONCE UPON A TIME . . .

THERE WAS A MATCHMAKER NAMED HARRIET

Who wouldn't like a fairy godmother, one who drops in, bearing just the right shoes, and providing classy transportation immediately before Prince Charming's ball? Isn't that what every single girl could use: a little divine intervention in the form of someone who both knows how to seal a match and comes bearing gifts?

Well, matchmakers in the non-fairy-tale world are usually a bit more mercenary. Now that the matchmaking business has become an industry, with certification programs and hair-raising fee schedules, we expect our matchmakers to be fashionable urbanistas, the type who can attract the guys and then, ipso changeo, deflect them on to us. Just check out the photographs in the back of many urban newspapers and magazines and you'll see the bleached teeth and botoxed foreheads of the American matchmaker, circa 2009.

But matchmakers can certainly come in all shapes and sizes, as our friend Doryne learned.

For Doryne, the strangely dressed woman with big red rouge circles on her cheeks, the one who seemed to loiter outside of the gym Doryne frequented in Fort Lee, New Jersey, was the least likely of fairy godmothers. But when "Crazy Harriet" approached Doryne and asked her if she was married, Dor played along. Harriet asked for Doryne's astrological sign and promised to fix her up with "a nice Jewish boy." Dor thought, yeah, whatever. You and all the rest of my mother's mah-jongg club, none of whom ever delivered.

But deliver Harriet did. Unfortunately, what she deliv-

(continued)

ered was not, at first, of the finest quality: "Six Pee-wee Hermans with dirty fingernails," Doryne recalls. What made Doryne stick around for number seven even she cannot now say. Maybe she was just *really* ready to meet someone. In any event, stick around she did, and Doryne's three children are the result of the lucky seventh blind date arranged by Harriet.

When, not long ago, Doryne attended Harriet's funeral, she stood up to say what an important figure Harriet had been in her own life and she set off an avalanche: several other women said that they too had been strangers whom Harriet had befriended and promptly married off.

"She really was a good soul, a guardian angel for all of us," Doryne says today with tears in her eyes. But how many girls had Harriet approached who weren't open to her divine intervention? As Doryne points out, "It's a numbers game, but you have to keep an open mind. If you do, it will happen."

Now, that's a fairy tale with a happy ending!

Rule #7:
It's Good to Shop Alone

Remember the movie *A Beautiful Mind?* You know, in which Russell Crowe played a super-hot schizophrenic math nerd? (Words never before in the same sentence: hot, schizophrenic, math, nerd). Anyhow, remember the scene where Russell, uh, we mean John Nash, uses mathematic game theory to figure out how to get a beautiful girl in a bar to fall for him?

We have a theory ourselves: if game theory really helped you get any guy you wanted, then we and a lot of other girls we know would be studying math as we speak.

Does game theory have anything to offer girls looking for a good date? We have no idea, but what we do know is that the lesson behind the bar scene in *A Beautiful Mind* is that if you go out shopping for guys in a big group, you are adding to your own competition. Plus, you're making it hard for guys to approach you.

If you go to a party, do laps, check out the whole room—and do it alone! Don't talk only to your girlfriends: you're in the

PERSONAL SHOPPER TIP: Take an *Eat, Pray, Love* trip all by yourself. You will surely come home with a wealth of great experiences—and maybe a boyfriend, too!

business of meeting and the impetus to meet is greatest when you are forced to do it, i.e., you are alone.

And if you take a class, go on a trip, or do anything else that can be considered husband-shopping related: *do it alone!*

Janice says . . .

I met Steve by signing up to take a class all by myself. There was no competition, no friend saying "I saw him first," and it forced me to talk to the other students, including Steve.

This may be a good time to bring up a few common dating foibles.

DATING FOIBLE NUMBER 1

Let us set the scene: you're lonely. A lot of your friends are happily attached. As a matter of fact, your single friends are dropping like flies. It's getting tough to find someone to hang out with on a weekend night. You're starting to get nervous.

Then it happens. A fabulous guy comes in to your life. He's funny and interesting and smart. Plus, so gorgeous. And yes, he's gay. But you are having a fabulous time with him. He makes a great "walker"—he shows up, well dressed and ready to go, to all your events. He's like a best girlfriend and a handsome husband all wrapped up in one. Except, of course, that he has no romantic interest in you.

Listen, we love our gay friends. But don't get caught up in hanging out with him exclusively—no matter how tempting it is. And tempting it will be! A great gay guy can be a diversion that will keep you from your goal: shopping for a husband. So make time for him, but don't spend Friday and Saturday nights with him, even if it means you have to go out alone.

Sorry. He'll get over it.

And so will you.

DATING FOIBLE NUMBER 2

You go to a bar every Friday night with your friends. You put a message on Facebook that you are going. Your friends Friendster their friends that they are going. Texts are flying, messages are whirling, and before you know it, you and your best one hundred friends are at the bar. Problem is, you know all these people— and you aren't dating any of them for various, well-established, and unlikely-to-change reasons.

So, why are you there?

Break away, fly solo, and see what happens.

You might actually meet someone.

HERE'S HOW TO SCORE ON THE MEET MARKET

The solo shopper brings home the best goodies.

Rule #8:
Your Mother and Your Friends May Not Be on Your Side

Did it ever occur to you that your mother might not really want you to get married? (And for the word "mother," feel free to substitute "father," "sister," or any other close family member.) No, she will never say this. She will never, ever admit that she doesn't want you happily married. In fact, she may not even *know* that she doesn't want you married.

But maybe she really doesn't. And maybe that's keeping you from getting out there and really dating.

Consider this.

Some families are very entrenched. They are dependent on one another for a lot of things, including socializing every weekend and annual vacations. And while they think the adult children should be off starting families, this really would upset the status quo in a way that would disturb everything.

So, although they will say that they want you to get married, they really won't, in their heart of hearts, believe it. Somehow, that reluctance will get broadcast to you and received by those nerve endings of yours that are super-receptive to family stuff. And it may keep you from dating.

Perhaps they'll criticize the guys you bring home. Or perhaps it will be more subtle—there just will be no place for these guys within the family circle. Beware. You might be a victim of those who love you most.

This isn't just a family thing. Your best friend? The single one? She probably doesn't want you to get married, either. At least not until *she* finds the right guy.

Do you get the idea? Your single infrastructure—all the people you hang out with and all the things you do—will be disturbed by the right guy coming in and shaking up the status quo.

Consider that these people might not want you to make progress in your husband-shopping endeavors. Not real progress anyway.

Once you see the problem, you'll be able to do something about it.

HERE'S HOW TO SCORE ON THE MEET MARKET

Be aware that those who say they have your best interests in mind may keep their own interests first, perhaps without even knowing it. So, the wise shopper shops for herself and herself only.

Rule #9:
Sorry, but . . . You May Need to Repackage (Yourself, That Is!)

If all the best shopping venues yield no results, you may have to look at *how* you've been shopping. In other words, it may be time to take a look at yourself and ask: "Is there anything else I can do to improve my dating odds?" We don't want to be finger-pointers, and we certainly don't think you have to turn into a supermodel clone to get a guy, but be honest with yourself, could you use a little sprucing up?

Answer this question: did you find a look in the last millennium that you just loved—and have you stuck with it ever since? Are cargo pants your be-all-and-end-all? Did grunge catch your fancy and have you not let it go? Or could you be a poster child for Banana Republic, circa 1998? Heck, even the biggest fashionistas among us can get stuck on a look and hold on for dear life.

Let's face it. A makeover can be a life-changing experience (or are we the only ones who TiVo all of the makeover reality shows?). It seems to us that a good makeover, a transforming one, can do almost as much as several extended visits to the therapist's couch. Once you see yourself as an attractive, youthful, fashionable person again, you'll have a new lease on life, not to mention a new lease on dating.

But because we can't all be featured on *What Not to Wear* we spoke to the author and style and makeover expert Stacy London herself to see what suggestions she has for those of us who can't (and probably don't really want to) stand in front of the 360-degree mirror in our undies and have the results broadcast on national television.

STACY LONDON'S GUIDE TO MAKING YOURSELF OVER, ALL BY YOURSELF

Stacy says a style makeover does wonders for a woman's self-confidence. It's all about reassessing your strengths and weaknesses and highlighting the stuff you love, while camouflaging the stuff you don't.

Dress to show how much you like and respect yourself,

(continued)

and dress to attract the company you want. Cover more skin if you want to hook a husband as opposed to getting laid. Wear a tight-fitting suit, not a tube dress. You don't want to look trampy unless you want a one-night stand.

Here are some specifics:

Jeans: Try on about twenty pairs. Good jeans should make your ass look great. Denim is never too intimidating—it's approachable. Go for the longest leg line possible in a uniform dark wash without bleaching or white spots. A medium waist is preferable to a low waist—muffin-top fat over jeans is no good! Men say they love the way a girl looks in jeans and a white T-shirt more than a sexy cocktail dress.

Old Trends: I don't care if you loved that suit from the 80s. You look like a schmu wearing it now. It makes you seem like you don't know what is going on today.

Color: Play up your eyes. You may think a guy is looking at your boobs, but on a subconscious level they see how bright your eyes look. It's a subtle way to put yourself out there.

And remember: *If you dress to your strengths, your self-esteem will go through the roof.*

But let's not stop at the clothes. Why not freshen up your makeup bag and throw out that blue eyeliner that's been there since before the first episode of *Seinfeld* aired? Here's the advice of Pauline Coutroulis, a television makeup artist:

CELEBRITY MAKEUP TIPS

Who to Talk To: Don't just ask your friends for makeup tips: consult a professional, someone who is objective and looks hip, current in both her attitude and her fashion sense.

Hair: If you want to add sparkle and refresh yourself, you have to use hair color: absolutely no gray hair is allowed! Highlights will freshen and subtract years from your face and, please, cut your hair every six weeks to maintain a polished look.

Makeup: Throw out everything you have! It's important to start fresh. You don't have to buy a lot, and less is more with age, but do get the best products you can afford and you'll see a difference. Buy a great makeup base that works with your skin type; cream eye shadow to lift your lids; a great, black mascara that's not a cheap one; and eyeliner that should be blended and smoothed out. And don't forget to wear lipstick day and night!

Skin Care: Take care of your skin and hide those wrinkles to the best of your ability! And don't forget the SPF.

Brows: Should be shaped according to the face shape and filled in. Thin brows make you look older.

You know, Stacy and Pauline got us all pumped up: as your personal shoppers, we really want to freshen you up for your husband-shopping spree. We suggest you go to your local mall and engineer your own makeover—without spending your vacation fund.

THE BASIC, HOW-TO-SHOP-FOR-A-HUSBAND MALL MAKEOVER

1. Makeup. Make an appointment—yes, of course they take appointments—at the makeup counter of your choice for a makeup application. Ask them to *teach you* how to do a face for day and for night. They may do one side and have you do the other side. Tell them you want something basic and neutral—a look that can be your new standard—and then buy what you need to replicate the look. After all, the makeover is *free*! So, be nice to the makeup artist, who works on commission, and nice to yourself, because you need a new look. Before you know it . . . aaaaah, now don't you feel better already? And don't forget to update your look periodically because this look, too, shall pass and you need to be up on the latest.

2. Hair. Now take your newly madeup face (seriously—we believe the better you look, the more inspired the hairstylist will be, so go made up) and head to the hair salon. Choose a good salon or use a stylist recommended by someone whose look you know is a good one. Put yourself in the hands of a professional and sit back. And don't be too controlling! Did you hear us? We said: don't be too controlling! That means don't look like you are going to cry if they cut off more than an inch. Take a chance and see what happens when you let a professional do his or her job.

3. Clothes. Give yourself a present. And make it a cash gift. By this we mean set aside a generous budget—

whatever you can comfortably afford—and put it in the hands of the personal shopper at a quality store in your mall. Tell her you need a date outfit and a work outfit, something flattering and up-to-date, but not too trendy. And don't be intimidated! After all, personal shoppers are women who work at a mall, not the Devil in Prada. And if it's your body that you are self-conscious about, remember that they see women of all sizes and shapes. And have you taken a trip to a Loehmann's dressing room lately? Everyone out there doesn't look as great as you think! Believe us, the personal shopper will not be appalled by you; besides, she gets paid on commission! So, once again, get out of her way and let her show you what looks good on you. You may be stuck on pencil skirts only to find out that A-lines are your thing. You never know! And if you don't get a helpful personal shopper, try a different one, or a different store. The mark of a good personal shopper? You should feel fabulous when they are done.

The mall makeover just may lead you to a newfound interest in taking care of yourself. Sure, there's plenty more you can do, once you get started: eyebrows and toning and facials and tanning and injectibles and on and on. But start with your makeup, hair, and, clothes: these are the essentials.

We think the mall makeover is an underutilized resource, one that is cheap enough to exploit on a regular basis. So, don't let your hair grow out for months and months, or let your newly purchased makeup lie fallow in the back of your bathroom vanity drawer. It feels good to look good, so give yourself the present of taking a little extra time and keep your makeup, hair, and clothes in good order. They are the basics of looking and feeling good.

One last thing, and this is a tip from behind-the-scenes of television studios everywhere. There is nothing, and we mean nothing, like a professional blow-out and makeup application. So, if you are going on a date about which you are hopeful (and why would you go on a date under any other conditions?), we say splurge—again, if you can—and go to the pros. In most cities in the United States, you can get a blow-out for thirty-five dollars and a free makeup application with the purchase of a few products. It's worth it. You'll feel confident and beautiful and that translates big-time into a fabulous date.

HERE'S HOW TO SCORE ON THE MEET MARKET

Believe us, the best-looking women out there know this one simple fact. It ain't easy looking good. It takes work, so get to it!

Rule #10:
Get Shrunk—
Yes, in the Head!

We are firm believers that if you are having serious trouble shopping for a guy—and by that we mean sustained, ongoing trouble—then you owe it to yourself to explore all options and to find out why.

"Therapists today work fast. We don't want to waste your time," says Laurie Weber, the New York psychologist. "We can get to the root of the problem and move you into the real dating world." So, how do you know if you need to place the call and get yourself on the couch? Dr. Weber says, "If, by twenty-three or twenty-four years of age you haven't had a relationship that lasts more than a month, or, if by your mid-thirties you haven't had a serious relationship, it's time."

Dr. Weber says that many girls have underlying issues that keep them from really entering the dating world. They may *think* they are dating, she says, but they are always with the same guy— the guy with whom they will never close a deal. The drinkers, the noncommitters, the older married men. If these guys are your "type" you are not really dating, says Dr. Weber.

PERSONAL SHOPPER TIP: Going to a shrink doesn't mean you are crazy. It means you know how to take care of yourself, body, mind, and soul!

According to the doctor, "Something may be blocking your ability to truly date, and you need to find out what that is. These issues are often from childhood. You may have lost a parent and don't want to get involved with men because you're afraid to lose someone you love again. If you find yourself picking men and you know—or should know—that the outcome is not going to be good, then you owe it to yourself to get to the root of the problem."

ANN CURRY:
A NAYSAYER?

"I don't believe you can shop for a husband," says Ann Curry, the *Today Show*'s lovely and charming news anchor.

Say what, Ann? Are you kidding?

No, says Ann, she's not kidding. "It's when you are not looking that the right love finds you. You have to be open to having acceptance in your life, acceptance of who you are and want to be. Then you are in a place where love can find you."

Okay, Ann, we'll give you a pass. Because we agree that when you strive to be the best you that you can be, and are open to it, love will—seemingly miraculously—fall into your lap.

Ann, who has been married for twenty years, says that a woman should ask herself some important questions to determine whether or not she has found the man of her dreams: "Fundamentally, do I respect him? Trust him? Love him? Does he feel all those things for me? A good marriage eventually evolves and allows you and your husband to feel so much compassion for each other. Each of you is worrying about the other. The goal is to feel supported."

That sense of being supported is key to the longevity of her marriage, Ann says. "What do I like about my husband? He prizes family. He invests much of his energies into making our immediate and extended family strong. And he is tender to me."

Ann also believes that she had a great role model when it came to shopping for—oops, we mean choosing— a husband: "I worshipped my father so there was a high standard of who a father should be. My husband meets that standard. That has made our marriage strong—his greatness as a father."

Let's face it. We are a generation that grew up with a lot of divorce, and researchers at UCLA say, "People whose parents divorced are at an elevated risk to dissolve their own marriage, compared to people whose parents did not divorce. We have to be careful in interpreting this—many people who come from a family of divorce go on to have successful marriages, and many people who do not come from a family of divorce go on to have marital problems—but it stands as an interesting and potentially important clue as we set out to understand and perhaps change how marriages develop." So if there is even a hint that your family history may be negatively impacting how you form and behave in relationships with the opposite sex—get to the root of the problem.

After therapy, Dr. Weber says she can see the shift: "When someone truly enters the dating field and isn't just repeating a dead-end pattern, you can see the change."

> For a marriage to be successful we must first recognize who we are—that we are a soul within a body. When you are at peace with yourself, when your body and soul are attuned to each other in fulfilling your life's mission, you are then in a stronger position to find your proper soul mate. When you don't yet know who *you* are, how can you possibly know what sort of person will be best for you to marry?
>
> **—Rabbi Menachem Mendel Schneerson**

HERE'S HOW TO SCORE ON THE MEET MARKET

Do whatever you need to do to become a real shopper and truly enter the dating marketplace.

Rule #11:
Don't Let the Last Seven Pounds, or any Other Lame Excuse, Hold You Back

Did you ever put off a shopping trip just because you needed to lose a little bit of weight—just a couple of pounds—before you could bear to stand in front of the dressing room mirror? Of course you have. And what usually happens? You never lose the weight and the need for the shopping trip turns from a casual "wouldn't it be nice?" to a dire "I have nothing, and I mean *nothing,* to wear."

Dr. Weber, the New York psychologist, tells us that "the last seven pounds—and for some reason it is always seven," is the number-one excuse she hears from her patients for not wanting to get out there and date. The same apprehension that keeps us from wanting to appear nude in front of the dressing room mirror also keeps us from wanting to appear, nude or not, in front of a prospective date. Dr. Weber says, "I always tell my patients just to get out there. Those last seven pounds are typically just an excuse they use because they are scared to put themselves 'on the market.' No one is seven pounds away from being datable."

Joy Bauer, the *Today Show*'s nutrition and health expert, agrees: "You never want to put your life on hold until you lose the last few pounds. Besides, it's easier to lose weight when you are out there and having fun. If you're inside and bored, you find yourself grabbing extra food and you'll never quite get there, anyway."

Okay, everyone pretty much understands that seven pounds is a lame excuse, even the girl who complains about those seven pounds, but some excuses are wielded with dead seriousness. Check out the following:

THE WHY-I-CAN'T DATE YET
HALL OF LAME EXCUSES

- I just want to lose seven pounds.
- I'm really too busy at work.
- I think my ex is going to come back to me really, really soon.
- I need to save up for some plastic surgery and then I'll be good to go.
- No one wants someone who has diabetes . . . or has had cancer . . . or has MS . . .
- I need to get through school first before I can start a relationship.
- My kids would be so upset.

- I think I'm going to move soon.
- I need to take care of my mother/father/grandparent.
- My dog hates men.

No, we did not make up *even one* of these lame-o excuses. And yes, some could almost bring tears to your eyes—but don't be sucked in. Each one of these excuses is lame and should be understood for what it is: a cooked-up reason to hide, due to fear of the big mirror in the dressing room of dating! Don't buy these reasons for not dating, ladies. Instead, accept them for the pathetic, vile, maudlin, bring-out-the-violins, lame excuses that they are, one and all.

How can we be so flip, you ask? So cavalier, so cold-blooded, you say? Well, don't you think women with sick parents, cancer, or men-hating dogs deserve to get married? We do! And we think these girls are perfectly marriageable as they are, right here and right now, and we challenge them—*and you*—not to use lame excuses to keep them, and yourself, off the dating scene.

PERSONAL SHOPPER TIP: Putting off for tomorrow what you should be buying today can lead to a shopping crisis! Don't wait till everything is perfect before shopping for a man. If you do, you may be waiting forever.

Listen, even the busiest among us needs—and has—some time to pursue their own goals and dreams, and the search for a life partner is a personal goal certainly worth pursuing. So, instead of spending your random night off with Mr. Dazs (you know, first name: Häagen?), get yourself out in that big pool of dating fun. Even if it seems a chore, you can't win it if you're not in it, right?

And if you would like to lose those seven pounds *while* you are out shopping for a man, fine. Here are Joy Bauer's tips for dieting and dating:

A PRIMER FOR MULTITASKERS:
HOW TO DIET AND DATE, ALL AT THE SAME TIME

Nutrition expert Joy Bauer says that while you are on a date, you "want to appear normal—you don't want to look like you are dieting." No one likes a restrictive calorie-counter, especially on a first date. Be sure to eat the day of your date, Bauer says, or you will appear lethargic, cranky, or worse: you'll have one drink and God knows what will come out of your mouth! In fact, you should never go more than five hours without eating.

If you follow Bauer's meal-by-meal dating and eating advice, she guarantees you won't have bad breath, feel bloated, or cause your date to think you're a dieting bore:

The Breakfast Date: Have whole-grain cereal, fresh fruit, and coffee.

The Lunch Date: Order salad with grilled chicken and low-calorie vinaigrette.

The Dinner Date: Order shrimp cocktail or a salad, grilled fish or chicken with vegetables, and skip the side starch. For dessert, order berries, or split a dessert with him and have just a few bites.

Other good advice from Bauer for losing those last seven, when not on a date:

1. Preplan what you are going to eat when possible so you don't just grab something when you are starving.
2. Go to the gym, because it puts you in a positive mindset and also because you won't want to muck up through overeating all of your hard work.
3. Snack on high-quality carbs and lean protein, a combination that will keep cravings at bay.

If you really want to meet a great guy, set your intention and don't let lame excuses derail you. Even busy, imperfect people deserve a significant other to love them. And so do you.

HERE'S HOW TO SCORE ON THE MEET MARKET

Don't let lame excuses keep you from shopping for your guy.

PART III

How to Close the Deal

Congratulations. You've met a guy. You knew what you wanted, you put yourself out there, and it paid off. We're so proud.

But how do you *really* know who he is and whether or not he's a keeper? And if things are looking good, how do you seal the deal?

We know. You thought you were almost there, but there's so much more to learn.

Fortunately, this is the area where consumer expertise really goes the furthest.

Why? Because shopping experts take no guff, that's why.

Now is the time to be relentless. When you are starting to really like a guy, logic and reason can fly out the door. It's like trying on that fabulous dress that makes you look skinny, skinny, skinny. You just have to buy it, no matter what it costs, right?

Wrong.

In the first two parts of this book, we told you to keep an open mind. In this part, we have to tell you the truth: you must be careful. Keep a critical eye open and make sure your guy is what he says—and you think—he is, because once we start to like a guy, our imaginations can start to embellish the reality that is him. We're here to tell you to stay smart, stay critical, and keep on top of your game.

Finally, when you know the deal is worth closing, we want to help you close it. But the terms have to be good. Don't sell yourself short and don't give yourself away for a song.

You're worth a lot more than that.

Rule #1:
Make Sure You've Done Your Research

Unfortunately, there is no Better Business Bureau or *Consumer Reports* when it comes to shopping for guys.

Not that women out there aren't trying to make up for the gap. Oh, no. There's plenty of dirty laundry hanging on the Internet clothesline. You need only check out LemonDate.com, The Dick List, CheaterNews.com and Don'tDateHimGirl.com to feel a lot better about your dating life. There are a lot of pissed-off women out there and they don't want to take it anymore! Furthermore, they are only too happy to try to spare you the pain. The problem is, these girls may just have an ax to grind. There's really no way of knowing.

Well, you don't have to resort to reading the slander sheets (not that we're opining on the legality of these Web sites, a matter that is being sorted out in the courts as we write) to find out the dirt on a guy. There are plenty of ways to get the scoop on a guy from sources that may provide a more balanced approach.

"Google is a girl's best friend." This is what one of our friends has to say about how to get the backstory on a guy you've recently met. Not that you'll find out everything through Google or similar search engines, but it will give you some context, and maybe some leads into finding out more.

And not just Google, of course. Facebook, Martindale-Hubbell for lawyers (oh yeah, Steve, Janice's husband was researched early on!), LinkedIn—they are all your best friends. Just keep in mind: most of these social networking Web sites are the creation of the people who supply the information. In other words, on Facebook you can put forward your best face, so don't take as gospel something that is a vanity production.

Some of the girls we talked to don't stop at the search-engine, social-network sites. They are members of background-check services, and they don't let a guy tell them who they are—they find out the real story. Background-check Web sites will tell you, for a fee, the story about a guy from his public records: marriage and divorce filings, criminal and sex-offender listings, along with addresses, house values, and the names of relatives and neighbors. Some of these sites specifically target online daters—and some online dating sites guarantee criminal searches have been made on all of their members.

We say it certainly couldn't hurt to find out as much as you can. Be wary, however, of the background-search sites: they reel you in with the promise of some information and then dangle the promise of more information—the really juicy stuff—for an additional fee. The costs can really pile up, so do your research

PERSONAL SHOPPER TIP: Do you know all there is to know about that man you want to buy? You don't want any nasty surprises, so do your research and do it well!

about these sites before you pick one and choose a level of membership that will give you some bang for your buck.

Naturally, a crop of specialized background-search services is popping up. HonestyOnline offers a certification system that attests to the accuracy of online profiles. Don't know what happens if he gains weight after he's certified at a trim 170 or joins a Hare Krishna temple after claiming to be an atheist. But it's one step closer to resting assured that you know just who you are dealing with.

Doing your research may mean being aware of the trends and scams that are out there. One astute shopper that we know was at a bar with a group of friends. A guy, pretty cute, approached her and seemed to be really suave, maybe too suave. In fact, all his "lines" seems so pat that she asked him, "Have you ever heard of Neil Strauss?" As you may or may not know, Strauss is a journalist who wrote the book *The Game: Penetrating the Secret World of Pick-Up Artists*. The book is about what is known as "the seduction community," an underworld of men who say they have cracked the code on getting women into bed with them. These so-called seduction artists use certain techniques and canned phrases that are purported to be irresistible.

BE PHILANTHROPIC:
COMMUNITY SERVICE THAT COUNTS!

Anna feels she is doing a public service. She has compiled "The Book," a rating guide to her very own Internet dating experiences . . . and she leaves it by her front door for all her friends to peruse. In "The Book" Anna includes printed-out profile pages for each man Anna has had contact with online and tracks the trajectory of each exchange. If the initial contact resulted in a bad date, all the gory details are right there in "The Book," ready to alert the next poor girl who may find herself on the wrong side of the dinner table with Mr. Yuck. On the other hand, if the guy was great, but just not Anna's cup of tea, then he receives a high score. Think of "The Book" as one girl's personal Zagat guide to her dating life.

May we suggest more books like this one? Share the knowledge, girls! In addition to being a wealth of information for all your girlfriends, a book like this could save you from the embarrassing situation in which you start an e-mail exchange with a guy only to realize, "Uh. I think I've been here before!"

We give "The Book" four stars.

Well, not! Our friend caught one of these pick-up artists in the act and left him, drink in hand, at the bar. Evidently, that guy underestimated the power of a woman who knows how to shop for a man!

Janice Says...

I was walking down 57th Street in Manhattan one day not long ago when a guy stopped me and slipped his business card in my hand. "I'd really like to go out with you sometime," he said. "If you're interested, call me." Well, he looked like a nice enough man, well dressed and well spoken, but I was, by then, married and the mother of a toddler.

Not one to let an opportunity pass, however, I thought of my friend Amy, a recently single television producer, so when I got back to my office, I e-mailed the guy and told him I had a great friend who was single. Would he mind if I passed his card on to her? Not at all, he replied.

Well, I told Amy about this man and she was all excited. Then I started to have second thoughts. After all, this was just some guy I met on the street—someone I really didn't know anything about!

I was telling another friend who lives in the neighborhood, about the situation. I told her the guy was a lawyer (his firm's name was on the card). She asked for his name. Would you believe it—she knew the guy! She also knew that he was a creep—notorious for having "women of the night" (i.e., the kind you pay for) visit his apartment at all hours!

Just goes to show you: ask around. It pays to do your research.

It almost goes without saying: when you buy a refrigerator or a car or a computer, you get the specs, not just from the salesman's mouth, but from a reliable, objective source. So, do yourself a favor and get the impartial facts on every guy you date. You owe it to yourself.

HERE'S HOW TO SCORE ON THE MEET MARKET

Who needs *Consumer Reports*? A smart girl can do her research in any number of ways and knows how to get the specs on any guy in the marketplace.

Rule #2:
Remember to Read the Labels Before You Put Him in the Wash

Most girls can get the scoop on guys they meet, be it through Google or friends or more inventive means. But uninterpreted, or misinterpreted, data is worthless, doncha think? And sometimes it's not just the hard-to-get information about a guy that we girls misconstrue. Sometimes, we simply fail to read what is printed right on the label—in plain English for anybody to see.

Case in point: our friend, a corporate attorney, met a guy who seemed not a little fabulous but really, truly fabulous. From his four-star educational credentials to his philanthropic job to his good looks and his cute Scottish accent, he had it all. Or so it seemed. When he stopped calling suddenly, after a series of great dates, our friend was blindsided. Where was this coming from? Then she realized, she hadn't read the labels. This guy was in his forties and had never been in a serious relationship until he married his first wife. And why did he marry his first wife? To get his green card. Sure, he liked the woman. Maybe he even loved her. But what forced his hand and made him, finally, commit? Only the threat of the immigration authorities. This guy's label said: NONCOMMITTER. DO NOT PROCEED. She just didn't read it.

PERSONAL SHOPPER TIP: It's easy to ignore the obvious when you really just don't want to see it. Try to separate out what you want to believe and what is true. There may be a chasm between the two.

Let's face it. Sometimes we girls just don't want to see what's clear as day. That's why the phrase (and the book and the movie) "He's just not that into you" struck such a chord with people. It's often the obvious, plain-as-day indications of lack of interest that we miss.

Why? Simply because it is painful to think that someone doesn't "get" us. The thought of being unappreciated or, worse, ignored, is simply intolerable. And so we begin to make up excuses.

It's the same thing we do when we get desperate to find an outfit for an important event. Maybe the big day is approaching and we think the dress in hand really "should" work. So, we start telling ourselves stories. Well, the belt isn't that bad, and the color is almost right, and the length can be tailored. Maybe we should just admit it: the dress isn't right. It's time to go back to the drawing board.

Quite simply, dresses that shouldn't be washed should go to the dry cleaner. Pants that shouldn't be ironed should be left

HOW TO KNOW THAT YOU ARE NOT READING THE LABELS

- If you find yourself making too many excuses, you are not reading the labels.
- If you find yourself unhappy on a regular basis, you are not reading the labels.
- If you don't want to tell your friends what he says or does, you are not reading the labels.
- If your friends and family all hate his guts, you are not reading the labels.
- If you don't feel like you can be yourself with him, you are not reading the labels.
- If you are living in a state of anticipation and agitation, with little to no satisfaction, you are not reading the labels.
- If your idea of him is better than the reality of him, you are not reading the labels.
- If you don't know where he stands, you are not reading the labels.

to hang dry. And guys who show you that they are not in it for the long haul, should be taken at their word.

Read the labels. They never lie.

HERE'S HOW TO SCORE ON THE MEET MARKET

Be sure you read—really read—the labels before you end up with a guy who falls apart in the wash.

Rule #3:
Dump These Guys

Let us guess. There's at least one article of clothing with the price tags still on it in the back of your closet, right? And a pair of shoes that looked great at the store, but are so uncomfortable, you never wear them. Also, you have had that "What was I thinking?" feeling about more than one purchase over the years. And, finally, you have, on a rare occasion, seriously overpaid for something and felt really, really bad about it.

No, we don't have a crystal ball. It's just that these are the classic pitfalls of shopping and everyone, at one time or another, falls for most, if not all, of them.

No, there is no way to ensure that you will love every purchase you make—no shopper is that good. But consumer experts can tell you how to minimize the chances of making a bad purchase, one that will inevitably cause you to feel that awful feeling known as buyer's remorse. Years of observing shopping behavior have allowed us to home in on certain scenarios—and certain scammers—that crop up time and time again and inevitably suck in the unassuming shopper.

Well, it's almost uncanny how these consumer pitfalls have their parallels in the dating world. Just as shoppers fall for the same rip-off scenarios time and time again, so do women make certain time-honored dating mistakes. Check it out:

THE IMPULSE PURCHASE

In the Shopping World: We've all done it. Maybe you were feeling a little down one day and decided that a shopping trip would be just the right pick-me-up. And so, even though you really didn't need it and hadn't given it much thought, you decide at the last moment to buy a dress, an unreturnable dress, only to bring it home and decide it is the ugliest dress you've ever seen. And it doesn't fit very well, either. Stores love the impulse shopper. In fact, they cater to her by placing all sorts of tempting items right by the cash register, ready to be grabbed without a second thought. Impulse shoppers do their buying on a whim, often to assuage a bad mood. They are not doing a lot of thinking.

In the Dating World: See the parallel? Of course you do, because you've been there, right? Coming off a bad relationship, feeling kinda lousy, depressed, alone in the world, there's a guy at the bar, he's cute enough, and before you know it you've had a few drinks and he's looking better by the minute. The movie *Knocked Up*? It's all about the classic impulse purchase, and while Seth Rogen always turns out to be a nice guy, the underbelly of the guy world also understands the impulse purchase. In fact, they position themselves right near the bar: the better to see who is throwing back one too many and is most likely to fall for their evil charms. They are the gum and overpriced tissues packages of the guy world. Forget them.

Our advice: Avoid the impulse purchase—it never ends well. Bring him home and you'll be flashing back to that year when you went shopping on the last day of Christmas and bought everyone on your list a Chia Pet. Instead of falling for an impulse purchase, shop in advance, use your head, and only go to the store when you are ready, and willing, to shop with care.

THE BAIT-AND-SWITCH DATER

In the Shopping World: Consumer experts know that "bait and switch" is one of the most insidious forms of fraud perpetrated on shoppers today. In the classic bait-and-switch situation, a shopper is lured into the store with the promise of an unbelievably great deal, only to be told that the deal is not available. But once the shopper is in the store a substitute is offered. It's not as great as the original deal that was advertised, but the shopper is either so disappointed that the original product is unavailable, or is simply lured in by the more expensive model, that she goes for the not-so-great deal. It's a scam and it happens all the time. Before you know it, you've got a computer . . . or a refrigerator . . . or a car that is a lot more expensive than the one you intended to buy.

In the Dating World: Bait and switch exists in the dating world, too. Ever meet a guy who is better than great at first? He's so cool and interesting and cute and he knows who you are—he sees you like no one has ever seen you before. You get hooked on how great his compliments feel, on how real the relationship seems to be. But slowly, over time, he seems to lose interest. You're no longer the most fantastic girl he's ever met, it seems, but you hang in there, trying to recapture the glow of those early, halcyon days. The real story? This guy is the classic narcissist, a guy who lures you in and loves you at first, only to become cold and rejecting when you cannot possibly live up to the exalted heights to which he originally held you.

Our advice: It's a classic—he draws you in with the bait of affection, only to hit you with the switch of his true nature, in all its cold and calculating glory. The bait-and-switch guy is a no-win scenario. We say it's time to move on.

THE TOO-GOOD-TO-BE-TRUE GUY

In the Shopping World: Janice's long-running CNBC show ended each day with the following advice: "It if looks too good to be true, it probably is." There's a reason this was chosen as the unofficial motto of the show. It's true! Fantastic buys often have hidden costs. For example, great financing deals look too good to be true because they hit you later with exorbitant interest rates. No one is giving anything away, so smart shoppers are wary of the deal that looks, well, perfect. Because, believe us, it's not.

In the Dating World: The classic too-good-to-be-true guy is handsome and polite and well mannered. He loves to do everything you like to do and he looks good doing it. He has a great job and a beautiful apartment and lots of friends. He's funny and makes a good living. And he likes to shop! Well, guess what? If you get all this in a guy, we're sorry to inform you, but someone has to do it: he's gay.

Our advice: A gay man is perfect in every way, except one. So if he seems too good to be true, have you considered the obvious? Maybe you should.

HERE'S HOW TO SCORE ON THE MEET MARKET

Avoid impulse purchases, bait-and-switch daters, and guys who are too good to be true. The consumer pantheon of nogoodniks translates to the dating world, too, so take our advice and steer clear of these classic consumer nightmares.

Rule #4:
Don't Fall for These Scams

Some scams are specific to the dating world, and husband shoppers worldwide need to be on guard. These scams have no names and, for that reason, are even more tricky to detect. Since time immemorial, a few bad men out there have been sullying the name of their gender with certain deceitful practices that will go down in infamy. Defend yourselves, ladies, against these conniving shysters and you will be a happier dater in the long run. Here is a guide that will help you detect these unnamed scams and sniff out a guy who is a bad buy.

SCAMS! HOW TO KNOW A SCAM WHEN YOU SEE ONE
He Doesn't Want to Have Sex with You.
Okay, have you noticed? Guys want to have sex. A lot. Especially young guys. If you are dating a guy and he doesn't want to have sex with you, there's something wrong and it's not your fault. If you're dating an older guy, he'd better be affectionate—at the

very least. If he's not, don't dwell on it, don't even bother to question it, and don't hang on. Just move on. It's a scam!

He Cuts You Out of the Vacation Photos that He Shows His Friends.

Who would do that? We don't make these things up, you know. You may think it goes without saying, but our friend didn't. So we'll say it: if you find out that he has shown pictures of your vacation to his buddies, but you were Photoshopped out of the pix, move on, girlfriend. He's up to no good. Don't dwell on it, don't even bother to question it, and don't hang on. Just move on. It's a scam!

He Goes on Mysterious Midnight Calls. Yes, He's a Doctor, but You're Wondering . . .

Yup, another real-life situation. Ask yourself: am I usually a paranoid person? Am I known to have irrational suspicions? Do I accuse other people in my life unjustly of crimes they didn't commit? If the answer to these questions is no, then trust your gut instincts. He's up to no good. Don't dwell on it, don't even bother to question it, and don't hang on. Just move on. It's a scam!

He's Never Been Married, but He Has a Beautifully Decorated Apartment. And He's Not "in the Arts."

Guys who seriously intend one day to get married don't invest in a big way in their bachelor pads. They just don't. If everything is perfectly placed, expensive, and he looks like he's staying . . . he is. Don't dwell on it, don't even bother to question it, and don't hang on. Just move on. It's a scam!

He's the King of the Booty Call but You Never See Him by Day.

Do you believe in vampires? If not, call it quits. Instead of the booty call, go out and buy new boots. Don't dwell on it, don't even bother to question it, and don't hang on. Just move on. It's a scam!

He Never Has a Real Job.

Sure, he's great in bed. He's romantic and interesting and fun. That's because that's his job. He's a professional boyfriend. His job is to have sex with you and have you support him. If that were your job, you'd be really good at it, too. Unless you want to support the guy for keeps: don't dwell on it, don't even bother to question it, and don't hang on. Just move on. It's a scam!

He Lost Your Phone Number.

Here's what Dawn, Janice's mother's friend, always says: "Even if you slam the door, if he really wants you, he'll come through the keyhole." And Dawn is right. Face it: it's pretty easy to contact someone nowadays. Almost everyone's e-mail address can be found in a few short keystrokes. If he really wanted you, he'd find you. If he doesn't find you, then don't dwell on it, don't even bother to question it, and don't hang on. Just move on. It's a scam!

He Has Ex-girlfriends from Every Member Country of the United Nations.

We like a guy who is not bigoted and who has friends of all different nationalities. But if, over time, you learn that your boyfriend's ex-girlfriends would make a lovely advertisement for

WHAT THEY DO WHEN
THEY REALLY WANT YOU

He lost your number? Puhleeze.

Jack saw his prospective wife, Miriam, for just a few seconds in a deportation camp in Germany after World War II. Both had been in concentration camps and were waiting to be relocated to the United States, but they never spoke. It didn't matter. Jack knew, at first sight, that he would marry Miriam. And so, in New York after debarkation, Jack spotted a friend of hers and said, "What is your friend's name and when is she arriving?"

Jack waited for Miriam's boat to arrive and approached her and her mother. Miriam thought to herself, "Who is this crazy guy?" and told her mother to ignore him. Well, mom knew better. She told Miriam that Jack seemed like a nice man—that she should give him a chance.

Miriam and Jack have now been married more than fifty years. They've had some very good luck and some very bad, including the loss of two children. But Miriam says, "I love him better today than ever."

Benetton or collectively look like the "It's a Small World" ride at Disney World, then we say . . . dump him! Why such an extreme reaction, you ask? Well, the guy with "exes of all nations syndrome" is a classic scammer: he is happy to hang out in the food court of dating, but he is not at the mall to make a purchase. Got it? He's just sampling, so don't dwell on it, don't even bother to question it, and don't hang on. Just move on. It's a scam!

HERE'S HOW TO SCORE ON THE MEET MARKET

Don't fall for a scammer. Just ditch him. You can do it!

Rule #5:
Let Him Think *He's* Doing the Shopping

Okay. You've steered clear of the scammers. You got yourself a pretty good guy. In fact, you think he's a keeper.

You've been dating for a while. You've met each other's families and friends. You've seen his hometown and been driven by his high school. You've had a major holiday together. You are getting serious and you think he's The One.

So, how do you behave if you want to get him to the register and hear the big ka-ching!?

Well, first of all, we can tell you what *not* to do:

THE HOW-TO-BE-A-GIRLFRIEND LIST OF DON'Ts

- Don't cook him dinner too often.
- Don't always be available.
- Don't nurse his every need.

- Don't give up time with your girlfriends.
- Don't neglect your family.
- Don't skip out on your job.
- Don't get too dependent on him.

Here's the key. You want him to think *he's* shopping for *you*.

We'll say it again, louder, this time, so listen: *You want him to think* he *is doing the shopping!*

That's what dating is about. Each one of you wants to feel as if you are doing the selecting and purchasing. It's human nature. Remember the speed-dating study that found that the worst attribute a woman could project was to seem unselective, i.e., desperate? So, project an image that *should* be the truth: you are a desirable item—someone every man covets but only one lucky guy gets to take home.

Here's how to think: you are to women what Manolo Blahnik is to shoes, what Chanel is to suits, what Ferrari is to cars. That's the idea. After all, these big-ticket items are wonderfully crafted, exquisite products. They don't have to try too hard because they are intrinsically great. So, know your own intrinsic worth. A great product is just great. If you believe it, he will, too.

PERSONAL SHOPPER TIP: You know you're a great buy, so let *him* have the pleasure of shopping for *you*.

If step one is changing your thought processes by believing you are a hot item, then step two is acting the part. In other words, don't discount yourself. Don't put yourself on sale mid-season.

How do women put themselves on the market at a discount? By allowing themselves to be treated poorly. In other words, try to keep the give-take ratio balanced in your relationship. If he's not willing to be exclusive, then neither should you be. If he's taking time to be with friends on weekend nights, so should you. If he's not showering you with presents, then what are you doing bringing him gifts?

We don't mean for you to go all tit for tat on him, but do keep in mind that your relationship should not be out of whack in the give-and-take department. If you are giving, giving, giving, he's going to think you're shopping for him, instead of believing that he is shopping for you. And that's just wrong, OK?

THE MAN'S PERSPECTIVE:

STEVE SANTAGATI

Steve Santagati is a self-styled "bad boy," but he is also exactly what every woman wants in a guy. Gorgeous, smart, a television personality, an extreme sports enthusiast, and best-selling author of *The MANual.* He even has a Web site, askstevesantagati.com, where he addresses dating problems. Need we say more?

So, when we decided to get a man's perspective, who better to ask than Steve?

Steve says: "Don't let him think you're shopping for a husband. It he gets an inkling that you are looking for a husband, he will go running."

It's like we said: make him think *he's* doing the shopping. We knew that, right?

What we didn't know is this: "You have to learn how men think. Learn their language," says Steve. "You are not marrying a human being. You are marrying a guy."

Okaaaay. So what does this species want? You may not want to know.

Steve says, "It is physical attraction that will bring the guy in. Make him believe you will be a fun person to be with and that you won't curtail his freedom in a negative way."

Does it all come down to looks and fun? Well, kinda. According to Santagati you must "bait them with your body . . . keep them with your mind. A guy that is going to love you for ten years is going to lust for you in the beginning stage the same way any guy would. It's whether you two have a bond and chemistry that will answer the question whether the relationship will get deeper. They weren't thinking in the beginning 'she will be my wife.' They were thinking, 'I want to slap her ass!'"

Oh boy.

Steve also says that you want to present yourself as someone who understands men: "We want to be understood by you so badly." And remember, "Set your

(continued)

boundaries. We will push it as far as we can go, just like an adolescent. In the end, we are just like children."

No problem, then. Women have been handling children forever.

So, what have we learned, ladies? We'll say it again, just because it is sooooo important: make sure he thinks *he* is doing the shopping. The easiest way to do that? Hold yourself out as a valuable purchase or, as a man might put it, make him want to slap your butt!

And remember you are couture, so don't think juniors, don't think bridge, and don't think misses. Hang yourself with the Christians (Lacroix and Dior, of course!) and he'll know he got the buy of the century.

HERE'S HOW TO SCORE ON THE MEET MARKET

Let him think he's doing the shopping by refusing to sell yourself cheap.

THE CHINESE ROUTE TO LOVE

Angel de Para is both a feng shui master, trained in Southeast Asia by Grand Master Yap Cheng Hai, and a recognized Buddhist lama, or reincarnated teacher of dharma, acknowledged by none other than the Dalai Lama. As a consultant to CEOs and celebrities, de Para is often called in to opine on the advisability of a love match. We thought we'd ask de Para what advice the ancient Chinese disciplines—feng shui and Tibetan Buddhism—might have to offer those of us out shopping for men in America today.

When you think about feng shui, de Para says, forget about those lifestyle shows on the design networks—you know, the ones where they put trickling fountains in the "money corner" and mirrors in the "love foyer." Instead, de Para says, think math: "Feng shui is the study of quantifiable data based on the energy of a date and geographical direction." Because feng shui is an esoteric science requiring years of training, de Para suggests getting the advice of a master—but only one trained in the classic manner, which, he says, eliminates many of the practitioners in the United States today.

Because finding a real feng shui master of your own is no easy task, de Para offers this advice for the rest of us:

First, know that, unfortunately, successful women often have bad luck in romance. The more luck in the money and fame areas a woman may have, the more chance she has of attracting infidelity, and the less harmony she may have at home. "Life is balance," says de Para, "so to improve your luck in romance, you sometimes have to go a little bit slower in the business world. Take things in stages: work on romance, then work on business, then go back to romance. I work with my clients in stages and let things level out before we move on."

Second, successful men also often have turbulent

(continued)

romantic lives. Those who attract money, says de Para, attract a lot more, including women, lots of women. "I advised one of my clients that if she married the well-known sports figure she was dating, things would not end happily." And so they didn't—boy, didn't they! According to feng shui, a more moderately successful guy in the worldly sense of money and fame may make the better husband. In any event, some matches are, in fact, more harmonious than others, and to find out which is which you need to know your "kua" number and his. "The more you study feng shui, the more you know what to expect and how to handle it," says de Para. (Shortcut to hiring a master: you can check out your number on one of many feng shui Web sites—it is based on your birth-date.)

Finally, de Para offers this classic Buddhist advice: "Desire creates obstacles." If you want something so badly, you will get in your own way. "Take your mind off the issue at hand. Sometimes I have to distract my clients by raising nonissues. If they really want a husband, I'll tell them they should focus on their health—that a problem may be imminent. Inevitably, they'll come back to me and tell me that when they weren't even thinking about it and were focusing on something else, a guy popped into their lives, seemingly out of nowhere. I'll tell them, of course he did. And I'll just smile."

Rule #6:
Check the Expiration Date

You would never even *think* of taking a big gulp from the milk container after its expiration date has passed, right? Eeewwww, of course not (maybe you'd never drink from the container at all!). Just one sour mouthful of dairy product is enough to turn you into a religious checker of expiration dates for the rest of your born days. Any smart shopper looks for the stamp on the carton before she leaves the store. Duh!

Unfortunately, men don't come with that handy "use by" date, although we are firm believers that they should. Hence, it is your obligation as a savvy dater to make the call yourself.

You've been dating for a while. You're convinced that he's your pick. But things are not moving in the direction you'd like. They're stagnating, stalling, and, quite simply, going no-where.

So, ask yourself: Is your guy going sour fast? Is it time to spill him down the drain and head back to the store for something fresh?

Some men are like fruit: they are a little green at first, but they ripen into a delicious juicy treat with time and care.

Others are like meat: they are best right from the store, the sooner the better—but they can rot before you know it.

In either case, there is risk involved: men are perishable and they can turn on you. So, what are the signs of an approaching (or passing or past) expiration date? When has a guy outstayed his shelf life?

First, we have to draw a fine distinction. We're sorry to do this, but we have to.

There is the "under-thirty-five-year-old situation" and the "over-thirty-five-year-old-situation." We're talking about your age here, not his.

Look. We live in a society with expectations and conventions, not to mention biological imperatives. The average age of marriage in America is twenty-six for women, and fertility rates drop markedly after the age of forty. It's a shame, because we'd all like to think we have all the time in the world, but take a trip through a fertility clinic and call us with your thoughts. We are drawing a line at thirty-five and we're sticking with it. Here's the scoop. Look for the signs of an approaching expiration date, but keep the following in mind:

Pre-thirty-five—If you are younger than thirty-five, you can give him a little extra time. How much extra, you ask? We don't know—use your judgment! Although the hallmarks of a guy who is about to rot are the same, you can give him a little more time to get used to the fact that he wants to settle down.

Post-thirty-five—If you two are thirty-five or older, you have to get serious. Be supersensitive to the signs of a guy past his prime (datingwise, that is) and be tough! Get out when the going is good (i.e., before you wake up and you are celebrating your fiftieth!).

If it is time for you to ask the big question, here are our guidelines for objectively assessing a guy's expiration date.

THE EXPIRATION DATE COUNTDOWN:
HE'S ROTTING ... AND IT'S GOING FAST ...

Still no talk of marriage, but:

... you're doing his laundry so often you know where all the permanent stains are.

... you two are starting to fight like siblings.

... his friends treat you like one of the guys.

... you can tell all of his stories for him, pretty much verbatim.

... you've met his whole family and they are starting to look at you with pity.

... the sex is getting a little, well, boring.

... at engagement parties and weddings, the innuendos about you two fly, with no visible reaction—other than chagrin—on his part.

... you have bought furniture together.

... when he goes, the bathroom door is sometimes left open.

Take note that part of the rotting process may be your fault. Yes, *you* can make him rot faster than he should.

How, you ask?

It's like leaving fruit out on the counter instead of putting it in the fridge. Sure, fruit tastes yummy if it's never been refrigerated and you eat it right away, but when left out too long, it is going to turn quickly.

PERSONAL SHOPPER TIP: If a guy has passed his expiration date, you have two choices: throw him in the trash or give him an ultimatum. The only wrong action is no action at all!

One way to accelerate his rotting process is by becoming too enmeshed with his family too fast. By virtue of your wifelike behavior, you will cause his expiration date to speed up. Why? Because wifelike behavior gets you taken for granted. Even wives really shouldn't display too much wifelike behavior. It'll get you ignored fast.

So, here's our advice:

DON'T GET TOO ENMESHED WITH HIS FAMILY BEFORE YOU GET THE RING

- Don't nurse his sickly mother.
- Don't hang his kids' artwork in your office.

- Don't give his teenaged daughter a loan or become her pal.
- Don't pose for Christmas cards together.
- Don't cook Thanksgiving dinner for his family and friends.
- Don't suddenly become best friends with his sister or cousin.
- Don't buy him presents valued at over $100 max.

Okay, you guessed it. These are real-life scenarios. We've known girls who have done all of the above, and more. It's very sad when that happens. It causes the guy to think the following awful words, words you never, *ever* want him to think: *Why bother?*

In other words, if he has it all right now, why bother going through the trouble, not to mention the expense, of asking you to marry him? Why indeed? So, remember this: until you get a ring, those are *his* relatives and *his* obligations. Not yours. You can be sympathetic and you can be kind. But don't get in too deep.

If you remain unconvinced and believe that the above-mentioned activities are just the kinds of things a nice girl should do, think of it this way. He is a balance sheet and you are an investment banker. Would you acquire his debts without acquiring his assets, too? No. That would be stupid, so don't cut yourself a bad business deal.

Here's the bottom line: if only one of you is playing "married couple," then you might as well take up solitaire. At least that way, you'd have the chance of winning once in a while.

HERE'S HOW TO SCORE ON THE MEET MARKET

Watch his expiration date. It may not be stamped on his forehead, but you can find it if you know where to look.

Rule #7:
If You Want to Walk the Walk (Down the Aisle, That Is), Be Sure to Have "The Talk"

"Honey, let's exchange credit reports. Please, baby? I just want to see your score."

Romantic, huh? Bring on the Barry White and the cheap chardonnay, because this is going to be one night to remember, right?

Well, romantic or not, according to Jean Chatzky, *The Today Show*'s personal finances whiz, these are the "little nothings" you *should* be whispering in your significant other's ear. It's not important until the relationship gets serious, says Chatzky, but then it is essential that you have "the talk"—the finances talk, that is.

When you begin to get serious about a guy, it's par for the course to meet his parents, visit his hometown, and learn about his high school exploits, correct? But Chatzky says that's not all you need to know: you also need to know whose financials are stronger, yours or his? Not only will this information allow you to balance power in your relationship—without anyone's sense of masculinity or femininity being mangled in the process—it will also allow you to forestall a potential catastrophe. After all, once you're married, *his* problems become *your* problems—bigtime. And if his credit score stinks, or if he has collectors nipping at his ankles, you're headed for your own personal credit crisis.

So, ask the hard questions, and if you get shady or vague or suspicious answers, take action. In Chatzky's opinion, "Financial dishonesty is a reason to break up. If you can't talk about money to the most important person in your life, then what else are you dishonest about?" We say amen to that. Nip it in the bud, girl! A short, painful relationship hurts like hell, it's true. But it doesn't hurt nearly as bad as a long-term relationship, involving children, mortgages, and joint bank accounts, that descends into financial misery. We've seen it, ladies: the woman who thinks her husband is at work when he's really hanging out in the local Barnes & Noble, afraid to admit he lost his job; the one whose husband has gambled away their kids' college funds; the wife who takes no responsibility for the family finances, only to be informed that her affluent lifestyle is a house of cards—one that fell last week. These scenarios are like having your own personal Great Depression, and they are certainly something to get depressed about.

So, have "the talk." Have it again and again.

The talk, after all, serves more than just one purpose: it's not just for smoking out a rat. Chatzky points out that talking about money brings up so many other issues: how hard you each want to work, how important spending is to you, how much freedom (or control) you need, and how honest you can be. She suggests that if you want to have a healthy marriage, you should have a financial discussion every week or two, just to keep things in check. After all, financial problems are a major divorce catalyst, especially in the early years of marriage.

Now let's get back to those mangled gender associations. Huh? You know, the situation in which you earn more than he does, or you come from a family that has more than his does. Sure, some guys have no problem with this state of affairs and will smile all the way through the nice vacations you bankroll and the better restaurants you bring into their lives. That's cool, as long as you're cool with it (and as long as he brings to the table his fair share in other, perhaps less tangible ways). But other guys still trail the remnants of machismo, even in these postfeminist days, and in their heart of hearts feel less than manly if they are the minor provider in a relationship. Yes, it's ridiculous, and no, you don't care that you have more and are only too happy to share. But believe us, ladies, this is an issue that needs to be discussed and discussed again, because it is one that can rear its ugly head years down the road with few hints that a monster lurks beneath the lovely façade of your marriage. We told you before that social scientists have discovered that marriages in which the man earns more outlast marriages in which the reverse is true. One way to counteract this outdated problem is, you guessed it, to talk about it. Talk about your feelings and talk about his. Air it all out and let it see the light of day—you may just solve, or forestall, any problems.

PERSONAL SHOPPER TIP: Know your budget—and his—before you make a purchase. And make sure your collective assets outweigh your debts, hands down!

One more thing about the talk: it has to be done well, with understanding and knowledge. So if you don't know anything about finances, grow up! If you're an adult, it's time to learn. We know, we know: many girls hate math, and, as a result, we women often don't take the time to understand investments and finances and don't enjoy talking about them. If this is you, get over it. You owe it to yourself to learn what a stock is, what a bond is, why you would invest in one and not the other, and when to do so. You owe it to yourself to understand your personal finances and share control with your husband once you are married. That way, when you have the talk, it is an educated, enlightened discussion, not just a fear fest or a self-recrimination bath. It'll be much more productive that way.

HERE'S HOW TO SCORE ON THE MEET MARKET

Before you close the deal—and very often after you close it—have "the talk," the one about money. Good shoppers know how to walk (down the aisle) and talk at the same time!

ONE WAY TO CLOSE THE DEAL:
BE DIRECT

Tracy, a public relations specialist, told us this story about her sister, Julie, who closed the deal in an unusual way.

Julie is notoriously organized. She's a girl with a plan, one who prefers, if she can have her way, to leave little . . . or nothing . . . to chance.

For Julie, marriage and kids were definitely in the picture. And in her mind, her boyfriend, Oliver, was "the one," so she took her calendar out and started planning. She picked a date upon which she would prefer her first child to be born, and then she backtracked. Nine months earlier, pregnant. Two years before that, married. Wait a minute, Julie thought. That means I need to get engaged. Now!

Rather than allowing things to naturally run their course, as most definitely is not her wont, Julie took matters firmly in hand. She made a plan. Actually, she called it a campaign. To wit: "Julie's Campaign to Get a Ring." But, Julie thought to herself, she needed troops, arms, a plan of attack, so she drafted an e-mail to her friends and relatives. Please, she beseeched them, contact Oliver immediately and tell him he really should ask Julie to be his wife. Now!

Well, the troops fell in line and Oliver began to get phone calls and e-mails. Lots and lots of them. All telling him the same thing: "You really should propose to Julie, Oliver. She's such great girl."

(continued)

You may wonder: did Oliver run? Did Oliver get so pissed off at this affront to his masculine decision-making authority that Julie quickly became history? Did Oliver nip the campaign firmly in the bud?

No. Oliver did what he was told. He asked Julie to marry him. And they are happily married to this day.

The moral of the story is: sometimes it pays to ask for what you want. You just may get it. Now!

Rule #8:
The Fine Art of
Closing the Deal

Negotiation is not just an art—it is also a science for some shoppers. They haggle not only when buying antiques at flea markets or Oriental rugs in Marrakesh but also when shopping at Tiffany and Best Buy. Smart shoppers know that bargaining can work just about anywhere and they make it a point to learn how to do it well.

The skills of a good negotiator are time-honored; they have been in play since the days of the Greek agoras. And luckily for us, the techniques used to close a deal in the commercial marketplace are pretty much the same as finalizing the most important shopping trip of your life.

So, here they are, the three golden keys to the fine art of negotiating, whether you are buying yourself a rug *or* a husband:

- You must arm yourself with the right information.
- You must be willing to walk away.
- You must be brave enough to ask for what you want.

Trust us, it works.

1. ASSEMBLE YOUR RESEARCH BY COMPARISON SHOPPING

The first step to haggling is research: your greatest tool is knowing the marketplace. After all, if you have knowledge—concrete knowledge—that there are comparable deals elsewhere, you can bargain anyone down. What do smart shoppers do? They bring an ad from a competing store and ask for a comparable deal.

How does this translate to the dating scene? Well, our advice is not to go exclusive with him until you are pretty darn sure he's the one. In other words, keep your options open—and keep going on dates and meeting people—until you can honestly say to yourself that he is marriage material (and it looks like he thinks you are the same).

There's nothing wrong with keeping the pipeline open until you know you have a keeper. If he's not asking you to stop dating other guys—and certainly if he's not giving up other girls—under no circumstances should you limit yourself. He's telling you that he's not sure yet. That means: he's not sure yet. Get it? He may be gone tomorrow, so don't start making sacrifices you might regret.

Come on: don't you sometimes buy more than one outfit for an important event and then return the ones you don't want when you've finally made up your mind? That's the idea here. Don't give up the right to compare deals until the deal in hand is looking really, really good.

And let's not ignore the jealousy factor because, ladies, it works. If he knows he may lose you to other bidders in the marketplace, it will light a fire under him. Competition makes your price rise. Hey, if you've got the laws of human nature and capitalism working for you, why not use them to your advantage?

In short, comparison shopping can be a beautiful thing.

2. BE WILLING TO WALK AWAY—AND BY THAT WE MEAN, DON'T MOVE IN WITH HIM!

Another tip from the annals of expert negotiators? Good hagglers know that when you negotiate, you have to be willing to walk away, or make the seller *think* you're willing to walk away. If you act too interested or eager, the game is over.

A smart shopper doesn't commit until she knows the deal is a keeper.

Yes: same with guys. The key to closing the deal is not giving yourself away without the quid pro quo from him: a commitment. And, yes, of course you can—and should—have sex before marriage (no, not on Date One or Two, but later, when things are literally and figuratively "heating up"). You just shouldn't move in—both because (a), he may start to take you for granted, and (b), after living together it gets really hard for you to walk away.

Did we just hear you say to yourself, "But I don't like to play games. Why should I play games? This is my life! And I like him. I want to live with him."

Was that *you* we heard?

Sigh. Did you hear us? We'll say it again: sigh.

That was us, shaking our heads in pity and just a little bit of exasperation. Yes, at you.

We beseech you: please get real.

Living together, although it sounds like a wise move, is a negotiating no-no. Grandma was right when she said, "Men who get the milk for free don't need to buy the cow." You may have rolled your eyes when she said it, but you were wrong and she was right.

Prove it, you say? Okay, we will.

According to Rutgers University's National Marriage Project, "The number of unmarried couples has increased dramatically over the past four decades, and the increase is continuing. Most younger Americans now spend some time living together outside of marriage, and unmarried cohabitation commonly precedes marriage." Sure, everyone is doing it. And it *seems* to make sense. As Professor David Popenoe, Ph.D., of Rutgers puts it: "The belief that living together before marriage is a useful way to 'find out whether you really get along,' and thus avoid a bad marriage and an eventual divorce, is now widespread among young people."

We all think it's true. We ask ourselves, how else will we really know if we can stand each other's vile little habits (the toilet seat issues, the milk-carton-to-lips habit, the long, permed hair in the drain problems) if we don't give playing house a whirl?

Well, here's the *real* truth, according to Rutgers:

"The available data on the effects of cohabitation fail to confirm this belief. In fact, *a substantial body of evidence indicates that those who live together before marriage are more likely to break up after marriage.*"

That's right: if you live together you are more likely to break up after marriage! What's more, a study at York University in Canada run by Anne-Marie Ambert, a sociology professor, found that *couples who live together before marriage "face as much as double the risk of separation as those who lived apart."*

Double!!!???!!

Sure, it could be that those who live together are just the kind of people who are more likely to break up later anyway. But the social scientists say that there is *no evidence to support the contention that living together helps you determine whether your marriage will work or not.*

And if he doesn't propose after you've been shacking up for a while, you'll always wonder: would he have bought the cow, if he couldn't get the milk otherwise? Would he?

PERSONAL SHOPPER TIP: Leave nothing more than a toothbrush at his place until you have a ring on your finger. Can you do it? Sure you can.

We asked our twenty-five-to-thirty-year-old cohort sample (OK—they're just a bunch of girls we know) what their thoughts are on living together. Their take? "If the relationship is going to work, it gets even better, but, inevitably, the sex gets worse." Huh! So in addition to possibly making him complacent and getting you entrenched in a relationship you can't easily leave, living together has another downside: the sex gets boring—and you're not even married yet!

So, do you get our drift here? Maybe it's not worth it, right? Why not just enjoy yourselves prior to the engagement and keep the romance hot?

And what about learning more about each other and getting to know each other well enough to make the decision to marry? We asked the girls whether they learned anything they didn't know about their prospective husbands by living with them. "No, not a thing." Didn't living together help them make up their minds? "No."

Then they told us the stories of their breakups. It's hard to move out, once you've moved in. It's painful and messy, and if you think just any breakup is hard, try breaking up after living together.

You don't want to do it.

So, our advice is this: don't move in unless and until he promises to love and honor you forever. *Then* you can move in with him.

Is that too much to ask?

We didn't think so.

3. ASK FOR WHAT YOU WANT

The final and most important tenet of good negotiation is to ask for what you want. It's as simple as that. You want a ring? You can ask him.

Okay, you say, but doesn't this conflict with your advice to always let him think *he's* doing the shopping?

We don't think so, and here's why.

You have to be absolutely sure that the shopping is over and done with before asking a guy to commit his life to you. You can, and should, ask him to marry you under these circumstances and these circumstances only: he has been given plenty of time to ask, and even though he hasn't done so, you *know* that he wants it but he just can't get his mouth to formulate those important—and, yes, scary—words.

So do it for him. Your girlfriends may say, "Oh, no, you didn't," but you just turn right around to them and say, "Oh, yes, I did."

Once you ask, you have to be willing to ride it out, because sometimes you have to wait for an answer. It's not easy, but it's worth it. At the very least, you'll know that you spoke your truth and stood your ground. And there's nothing wrong with that.

Janice Says . . .

After three months of dating, I looked at Steve and said, "Is there really anything more we need to learn about each other, or do we know everything we need to know, right now?"

He was in shock—no one else had ever spoken to him in such a direct way. But I knew he was it for me and I knew we had all the information we needed. I think I frightened him, though, because he didn't call me for about a week. It didn't take him long to realize the error of his ways, though, and looking back on my point-blank declaration today he says, "Thank you for making—and saving—my life."

Like mother, like daughter. After dating him for several years, my mother gave her second husband, Sid, an ultimatum: it was time to tie the knot. Just like Steve, Sid got scared at first, and they broke up. But my mother was glad she had put her foot down: "I said my piece and in the end, I probably saved myself some time." As soon as he went back to the *New York* magazine personal-ads scene, Sid realized what he had. He called my mother and said, "It was making me sick to be apart." Mom took

(continued)

him back, but by then she wasn't so sure *she* wanted to get married. The tables had turned and it was Sid's turn to beg. He said, "Please, my mother really wants us to get married!" Mom was still on the fence until one day she woke up and had a revelation, "Let's get married today." They went to the local county courthouse, had lunch afterward at a deli across the street, and are still happily married years later.

Sometimes, gut instinct and a few months of dating are enough to tell you a lifetime's worth of information about a person.

It was enough for us!

Asking for what you want can be a win-win strategy that will take you to the register fast. Tell him like it is: "Honey, the shopping is over. Let's put it on a credit card, keep the hangers if you'd like, and just throw the receipt in the bag."

It's time to head out of the store.

HERE'S HOW TO SCORE ON THE MEET MARKET

Negotiate your way into a happy marriage. Arm yourself with information about the marketplace, be willing to walk away, and ask for what you want. He'll be in the bag before you know it.

Conclusion . . . Or, How to Enjoy Your Purchase!

It may seem counterintuitive, but we find it to be perfectly logical: if you want to learn how to stay married, just ask a divorce attorney. After all, who knows how to do marriage better than someone who sees, day in and day out, all the stuff that can make it go wrong? So, for our last bit of advice to you, we offer the following words of wisdom, straight from the mouth of Suzanne Bracker, divorce attorney to the stars.

Esq. Bracker, who has been called the "blond avenger," says that it is a commonly held *mis*conception that marriages fail because of the triumvirate of sex, money, and in-laws. Not so, she says. According to Bracker, marriages fail for other reasons.

Interesting, huh? It's not the desire for a little somethin' somethin'. It's not bankruptcy, cancer, or random acts of God. It's everyday interactions of the ugly kind and lack of common decency than can send people running for the return line.

If these are the reasons marriages really fail, what can we do

THE LESS-THAN-TEN-ITEMS CHECKOUT LINE

...OR HOW TO GET DIVORCED IN SIX EASY STEPS

1. Lack of kindness and consideration
2. Verbal abuse
3. Failure to validate one another
4. Differing game plans
5. Substance abuse
6. Control issues

to be proactive? How can we take care of our purchases so that they last a lifetime?

Well, here's Bracker's insider advice, the kind that only a divorce attorney can give:

1. JUST BE NICE

Bracker says it is the mundane, everyday acts of inconsideration that lead people to pull the plug on their marriages. "Number one is that people complain of day-to-day lack of kindness and consideration. Women say the man doesn't come home on time. Men say that Father's Day wasn't celebrated." It's these small failures, these indications that the spouse is simply not a priority, that add up to marital disaster. What can we learn from this? Well, in the first place, be sure to pick a guy who remembers your birthday, who calls when your mother is in the hospital, who lets you know in advance if he can't make a date. Of course,

How to Shop for a Husband

we are expecting you to use common sense when applying this, ladies: no pouting because he doesn't remember the anniversary of your first kiss. And don't forget the vice versa: be a nice wife! Treasure and appreciate him. Make him feel like he's the great buy that he undoubtedly is. (He must be, if you got him after reading this book!) Build him up, buttercup baby, and don't let him down. Coddle him like a pair of shoes that cost you a paycheck. Okay? Do we need to explain further how to do that? We didn't think so.

2. DON'T BEAT HIM UP WITH WORDS

Bracker advises as follows, and we wholeheartedly agree: "Don't be stupid or say whacky things that just fly from your lips. People have memories that are really long." So true. Don't say anything in the heat of passion (the bad kind of passion) that you will regret later. If you are the type of person who flies off the handle and can't help but blurt out stupid stuff, work on this problem and fix it. Consult a therapist, a meditation expert, a religious leader, whatever!

The word "divorce" should not be utilized at all, throughout the duration of your marriage, except with respect to other people. Example: "Joe and Jennifer are getting divorced, did you hear?" That's allowed. Otherwise, put that word (d . . . d . . . d . . . ivorce) in the verbal-garbage/tantamount-to-abuse category. No fights in which you yell, "I'm calling my mother and telling her I'm filing for divorce." No screaming in the heat of the moment: "So what are you telling me, that you want a divorce?" No. No, no, and no. After all, you can't really enjoy a new dress if you're thinking of returning it, can you? We'd rather you

PERSONAL SHOPPER TIP: Here is a secret nugget of marriage wisdom, a bit of advice that we should really charge extra for, but we won't: *Unless you are ready to go the distance, don't ever threaten to divorce him, and don't ever ask him if he wants to divorce you.*

call him a jerk, an idiot, and the biggest moron you've ever met. But don't use that "D" word. Got it? This tip is essential to enjoying a happily married life. You can thank us later.

3. TELL HIM HE'S GREAT!

Suzanne Bracker told us a story about an Academy Award–winning actor (we wish we could tell you his name, it's a really good one, but we're sworn to secrecy) who divorced his wife because, despite his remarkable success, she could only find fault with him. He would get a role that he loved and she would say, "That's all you're getting paid?" Well, guess what? His secretary thought he hung the moon and had no problems with the money he made. So, he married her. The moral of the story? Even Oscar winners need to be told they're great . . . and told . . . and told . . . and told yet again. That's the deal, ladies. Men need to know you value them and need to hear it repeatedly. Call them little boys, call them insecure, call them whatever you'd like. (We've called them all that and more!) Just tell them they're great and that you love them. Often. Or they'll find someone else who will.

4. HAVE A SHARED GAME PLAN

Now that you are an educated shopper, you won't make this mistake. But because Suzanne Bracker says it is her number four most important bit of advice, here it comes again: make sure, in advance, that you share a common game plan with your husband. This means you essentially agree on where and how you will live and whether you will have children. You don't have to agree on everything, and you don't have to prognosticate the future with unearthly accuracy, but you do have to be generally on the same page. Otherwise you will end up in Suzanne Bracker's office saying, as so many of her clients do, "We just never discussed it." That would never happen to you, right?

5. AVOID SUBSTANCE ABUSERS

Sometimes you just can't predict it. We have seen it, ladies. You know, the forty-year-old who starts abusing prescription drugs for the first time in his life? It happens, and there's nothing you can do about it. But, on the other hand, sometimes you *can* predict it, so be honest with yourself. If a guy has a substance abuse problem that is unchecked (and by that we mean it isn't completely arrested or under control—as assessed to the best of your ability), then hit the road. Please. Otherwise you are in for a difficult marriage and a possible trip to the divorce lawyer.

6. LEARN TO LET GO

Suzanne Bracker says that an overbearing spouse's failure to let his or her significant other breathe is the number six reason people divorce. "What did you do today? What time was that meeting? Who was there? Why didn't you call?" That's the unpleasant sound of a wife (or husband) with control issues. "Some people are just too much," opines Bracker, "and they need to learn to back off." If you don't let him leave the house without an interrogation . . . or if he doesn't let you buy kitchen towels without him . . . your marriage may be headed for trouble. Don't fall for a control freak, and if you are one yourself, deal with the underlying issues and make the necessary changes. Otherwise, we see a divorce court in your future.

PERSONAL SHOPPER TIP: Talk to a divorce lawyer to learn the marital mishaps that cause people to take a long, hard look at their purchase and hightail it back to the store, receipt in hand!

Ladies, you are now graduates of the School of Husband Shopping. We're sorry to see you go, but we know you are ready to find a buy that your friends will envy and your mother will kvell over (that means she'll be happy—really, really happy). Please take care of your purchase. Treat him with respect and love and he will certainly return the favor. We're sure about that because you are now officially a consumer queen, a shopping siren, a maven of manly affairs. And we wish you all the best.

ENJOY YOUR PURCHASE! HAVE A NICE DAY!

The How to Shop for a Husband Dating Glossary

CLICK ADDICTION—A disease that manifests itself only online and is characterized by a compulsion to continually and unceasingly search online profiles for that mythical and completely imaginary creature know in the vernacular as "the one."

CONSUMER QUEEN—See maven of manly affairs.

DRESSING ROOM OF DATING—The place and time where you try on guy after guy, with no trip to the register in sight.

FOOD COURT OF DATING—The place where you go to sample the cuisine (and it's often fast food) and *not* make a purchase. A one-night stand is a trip to the food court of dating—it's not a serious shopping trip.

GIFT WITH PURCHASE—The in-laws, of course!

GIRL GHETTO—Those professions filled with women . . . and maybe two gay guys.

GOOD GUTS—The mechanics or basics that make a guy worth purchasing. The qualities you don't compromise on.

GUI OR GOOD USER INTERFACE—Good communication skills in a guy.

KA-CHING!—The proposal. The one you want to accept, that is.

LITTLE BLACK DRESS AMONG MEN—A guy who is a keeper; one who is going to last.

MALL MAKEOVER—What you need to do now, to update your makeup, clothes, and hair, to get you pumped for your husband-shopping spree.

MAVEN OF MANLY AFFAIRS—See shopping siren.

MEET MARKET—The dating marketplace.

MEN'S DEPARTMENT—Places where the boys are; locales where men are to be found in critical mass.

MIRROR-IMAGE RULE—The dating rule that says that the best mate for you is one who is most like you, in any and all of the following: looks, wealth, social status, educational level, family background, and personality traits.

ONE, THE—You'll know him when you see him. Caveat number one: that doesn't mean you won't have your doubts and get nervous—really, really nervous. Caveat number two: there's not really just one "the one," but there should only be one "the one" at any given time. Kapish?

OPTIONS—The extras that you are looking for in a guy. They can include anything from a love of the movies to a passion for skiing. They round out your PGHM shopping list and make it your very own.

PGHM—Perfectly Good Husband Material. A guy who is good enough—by which we mean really good—to bring to the cash register.

PGHM METER—Our take on what really counts, on a scale of 1 to 10, in making a guy a good buy.

POWERFUL ENGINE—Good sexual chemistry in a relationship.

RETURN LINE—You know. It starts with a D? And ends with an E? And the middle letters are IVORC?

SECONDARY MARKET—The dating market for second (or third, or fourth . . .) marriages: yours, his, or both!

SERIAL SEARCHERS—Online daters who are never satisfied and are always convinced that the perfect man or woman is just one more click away. (Syn.: Click addict; see Click addiction)

Westfield Memorial Library
Westfield, New Jersey

SETTLING—A no-no as far as we are concerned. Don't do it. But you should learn that compromise is *not* a bad word.

SHOPPING SIREN—You, after reading this book.

TALK, THE—The discussion about finances. The one in which you both spill all.